Seeing Together

Mind, Matter, and the Experimental Outlook of John Dewey and Arthur F. Bentley

By Frank X. Ryan

AMERICAN INSTITUTE *for* ECONOMIC RESEARCH

Great Barrington, MA

Seeing Together
Mind, Matter, and the Experimental Outlook of John Dewey and Arthur F. Bentley

Economic Bulletin, Vol. LI No. 11 November 2011

Published by:
American Institute for Economic Research
Economic Bulletin
250 Division Street
PO Box 1000
Great Barrington, MA 01230
888-528-1216
info@aier.org
www.aier.org

Economic Bulletin (ISSN 0424–2769) (USPS 167–360) is published once a month at Great Barrington, Massachusetts, by American Institute for Economic Research, a scientific and educational organization with no stockholders, chartered under Chapter 180 of the General Laws of Massachusetts. Periodical postage paid at Great Barrington, Massachusetts. Printed in the United States of America. Subscription: $59 per year. POSTMASTER: Send address changes to *Economic Bulletin*, American Institute for Economic Research, Great Barrington, Massachusetts 01230.

Editor: Marcia Stamell
Copy Editor: Sarah Todd

Book Design and Production: Jonathan Sylbert
Cover: Eric Taylor

ISBN 13: 978-0913610-79-4

Printed in U.S.A.

Preface

Life is mostly about what's next: the water bill, the ringing phone, a kiss good-night. We seldom stop to think about the past or the future. More rarely do we contemplate the big picture of who and what we are in this world.

According to Socrates, philosophy is a tool that helps us examine our lives. The philosophy introduced in these pages, *transaction,* is a radical extension of this idea. Whereas traditional philosophies separate the examining mind from the thing examined, transaction "sees together" as dynamically interdependent *what* we know and *how* we come to know it. The world is not a cosmic mind or spirit, as philosophical rationalists believe. Neither is it mere physical matter passively perceived by human observers, as empiricists insist. Instead, mind and matter together constitute our world and what we can learn about it.

The transactional approach is not new. Aristotle taught that reality consists of the unity of ideas and matter he called "formed matter." In the 18th century, Immanuel Kant reconciled empiricism and rationalism by demonstrating that our recognition of objects combines the senses and the intellect. His successor, Georg Wilhelm Friedrich Hegel, regaled the gradual liberation of intellect from sense as the ultimate destiny of the world.

American pragmatists Charles S. Peirce, William James, and John Dewey pioneered a contemporary theory of transaction. Dewey, in particular, envisioned mind and matter as jointly integral to a scientific and experimental outlook. Mind, for Dewey, involves the utilization of cultural resources to successfully resolve problems. Matter is akin to "What's the matter?"—the diagnosis of a problem at hand that leads to concrete efforts to resolve it. An object is the attained objective of problem solving, which literally incorporates the joint contribution of mind and matter.

Dewey's emphasis on experimental flexibility impressed Colonel E. C. Harwood, founder of the American Institute for Economic Research. This book explores the intellectual heritage of an economic methodology now included in the curriculum of AIER's summer program. Relevant concepts are explained as needed, and an attentive reader with no background in philosophy should be able to follow the argument as it unfolds.

Make no mistake, however, there is an argument here; this book is no mere summary or exposition. Late in life Dewey and collaborator Arthur F. Bentley confessed to promoting a "radical heresy" unappreciated, not just by foes but by many fellow pragmatists alike. They worked tirelessly to reinvent familiar but misconstrued concepts, including "transaction" for "interaction" and "cosmos of fact" for "experience," and to chart the progress of transactional thinking in the natural and social sciences.

Beyond introducing the transactional view, this book clarifies and defends this project as an invitation to re-imagine pragmatism, and indeed philosophy itself.

I wish to express my deep gratitude to Daniel Palmer, Elias Khalil, and Charles Murray, who spearheaded this project more than a decade ago; to John Shook, Jim Garrison, and Shane Ralston for their valuable help in shaping and articulating the transactional view; and to D. Wade Hands, Alex Viskovatoff, and Steven Cunningham for their insights into economics. I appreciate the support of my family, colleagues at Kent State University, and especially the tireless efforts of Marcia Stamell, Walker Todd, Sarah Todd, and Jonathan Sylbert at the American Institute for Economic Research for making this book a reality.

—Frank X. Ryan, Kent, Ohio , November 2011

Contents

1

Introduction

When we try to pick out anything by itself, we find it hitched to everything else in the universe. John Muir

A "real world" that has no knower to know it...has just about the same "reality" that has the palace that in Xanadu Kubla Kahn decreed.... A knower without anything to know has perhaps even less claim to reality than that. John Dewey and Arthur F. Bentley

Even pressed in a slide and inert, a butterfly wing is an amazing work of nature. Under modest magnification, thousands of colorful scales made of tiny overlapping plate-like hairs burst into view. Iridescent colors dazzle the eye—ideal for attracting mates and warning predators that its bearer isn't tasty. Yet what we might learn from a mounted specimen is dwarfed by what is not revealed. We can't witness, for example, the coordination of four wing segments in the figure-eight pattern that enables flight or the strong thorax muscles that choreograph this intricate ballet. We can't experience the capillary contractions that circulate oxygen or inflate the wet and crinkled wings that emerge from the pupa.

Reflective scientists and philosophers have long puzzled at the irony of dissection—that one must destroy life in order to know it. Still, it's been a mainstay of scientific practice for four centuries that complex phenomena must be broken down into basic components, then reassembled—like a machine— into a set of interacting parts. It wasn't until the middle of the 20th century that ecology, a term coined by Ernest Haeckel a century earlier, became widely accepted as an alternative to the mechanical view of life. Today, ecology often means a "green" mentality or a commitment to preserving nature. But this is only one potential application of a broader world view in which the basic unit of study is not a set of parts or even an organism. Instead, an ecological perspective opens itself to a complete bio-system of interdependent organisms and environments, including the interests and expectations of the one doing the exploring.

The comparatively late arrival of an eco-centric view is not hard to understand. It's easier to kill something and take it apart, easier to determine whether something is a mammal or a marsupial by examining organs or genetic signatures. To coordinate a complex web of behaviors takes much more work. Where dissection encourages instant classification and pigeon-holed conclusions, ecology counsels extended observation and findings that are tentative and revisable.

Given that physics and chemistry were the first sciences to liken organisms to machines, it's surprising that these hard sciences were also the first to embrace the ecological view. Seventeenth-century Newtonian dynamics understood heat, formerly regarded as a substance, as the interaction of discrete particles. In the 1870s, however, Scottish physicist James Clerk Maxwell challenged the notion that energy consists of an aggregate of distinct interactions. Instead, he looked toward a statistical configuration of molecular ranges within the entire system.

The Maxwell-Boltzmann distribution, as this is called, was generalized in the 1920s when physicists found themselves puzzled by so-called quantum effects, such as the curious fact that an attempt to fix the position of a particle increases the uncertainty of its trajectory. Viewed as the interaction of individual particles, each particle has a discrete position and trajectory, though the very attempt to measure these with, say, a photon of light, creates a disturbance that renders the measurement inaccurate. The prominent physicists Niels Bohr and Warner Heisenberg, however, rejected this entire perspective. They saw no reason why the micro-world must mirror the "billiard ball" interactions we perceive among the objects of ordinary perception. Instead, the available evidence supports the dynamic trade-off of position and trajectory as a function of the overall field, including the interests of the observer. This "radical revision of our attitude as regards physical reality," as Bohr put it, is now the consensus view among physicists.

The behavioral and social sciences have been more hesitant to contemplate the eco-centric view. Most of us still think of ourselves as spirits or souls inhabiting a material world, albeit a world where Freudian ids and egos now lurk beneath our surface personalities. We affirm "self-evident" truths at the expense of broader observations that entertain a variety of perspectives and an appreciation of historical and cultural crosscurrents. We tend to see, as did the philosopher Thomas Hobbes (1588-1679), an irreconcilable power struggle between haves and have-nots instead of relationships of interdependence requiring both individuality and cooperation in order to flourish.

Philosophy, which prides itself as the mother of the natural and social sciences, has been strikingly recalcitrant. Traditionally, philosophy's raison d'etre has been the search for immutable truth, the quest for certainty. There is, naturally, no agreement about what would constitute such a secure foundation. Some hail the Will of God or the axioms of logical and mathematical reasoning. Others look for conditions by which our sense experiences "hook into" the external world in a reliable way. To preview two key terms that Dewey used, such approaches are, respectively, *self-actional* and *interactional*—that is, they see knowledge either in terms of self-evident truths or as decoding the secrets of the external world.

Is there a broader, more ecological perspective? One viable candidate was developed over seven decades by the American philosopher John Dewey (1859-1952). Even as a child in Vermont, Dewey yearned to "see together" what other philosophies had set apart in opposition: mind versus matter, self versus object, fact versus value. Adopting an ecological stance long before the term became common, he was the first to test it in developmental education. Dewey founded an experimental school at the University of Chicago in the 1890s dedicated to replacing rote memorization with creative problem-solving in a social context. Later, at Columbia University, he gained prominence as America's foremost pragmatist, a term mischaracterized as settling for practical expediency when Dewey actually endorsed long-term solutions to recalcitrant problems. He called his approach "experimental idealism" and "naturalistic humanism" before settling upon *transaction* in the early 1940s.

In the last phase of his illustrious career, the aging yet vibrant pragmatist found a collaborator in Arthur F. Bentley (1870-1957). Bentley introduced himself by letter to Dewey in 1932 as having sat at the "outer edge" of one of his Chicago classes three decades earlier. Bentley arrived in Chicago having studied economics from a historical and cultural perspective at the University of Berlin, an opportunity unprecedented for an American at the time. His teachers, Adolph Wagner and Georg Simmel, believed that a human "self" is created in interpersonal relations, a view Bentley found resonant with Dewey's work.

Unable to secure a lasting teaching position after graduation, Bentley became a newspaperman and editor in the rough and tumble world of Chicago journalism—a better education in pragmatism, no doubt, than anything he might have learned in a classroom. He published *The Process of Government* in 1908, today a cult classic for its farsighted grasp of interest groups and pressure politics. Retiring at 40 to a leisurely life growing apples in Southern Indiana, Bentley found ample time for more esoteric studies, and he included a copy of his recently published *Linguistic Analysis of Mathematics* with his introductory letter to Dewey. Dewey's reply praised the work as having given "me more enlightenment and intellectual help than any book I have read for a very long time." Thus began a 20-year collaboration that ended with Dewey's death in 1952.

Dewey developed his vision of pragmatism and experimentalism in the first two decades of the 20th century. During the 1920s, regarded by many as his golden era, he produced masterpieces such as *Reconstruction in Philosophy, Human Nature and Conduct, Experience and Nature,* and *The Quest for Certainty.* With the onset of the Great Depression, Dewey turned more intensively to social and political themes, though he produced an important book on aesthetics, *Art as Experience,* and a complex work on the experimental and social nature of human reason in *Logic: The Theory of Inquiry.*

Dewey and Bentley saw their collaboration as an opportunity to place a capstone on the *Logic* by investigating the nature of sign-behavior. From primitive grunts and gestures to highly abstract theories, humans learn about themselves and their world through socially ingrained acts of communication. In search of reciprocal patterns between signs and sign-users, Dewey and Bentley had three specific objectives. First, they wanted to rectify misconceptions about Dewey's worldview caused by his careless use of *interactional* language in previous writings. They hoped to make it clear, for example, that organisms and environments are transactionally interdependent: a far more radical claim than the commonplace notion of separate things that merely interact. Secondly, they planned to create a lexicon of what they dubbed "firm names"—definitions that express the transactional view with greater precision. Finally, they wanted to develop a comprehensive theory of sign-behavior ranging from simple cues and gestures to the complex language of science and mathematics.

The Dewey-Bentley collaboration produced a series of articles published as *Knowing and the Known* in 1949. Though the distinguished octogenarians were praised for their remarkable energy and vigor, the book was not well-received. Dozens of drafts exchanged for each chapter make the work feel choppy. Bentley obsesses with minutia and the urge to shoot one-line refutations at *every* other point of view. Worst of all, though famous for deriding pretentious philosophical systems, Dewey builds a decidedly systematic theory of his own in *Knowing and the Known*. One critic, Paul Cress, went so far as to liken Dewey and Bentley to "lost mariners" who had "thrown the compass of reason over the side as so much excess ballast."

In terms of style and organization, *Knowing and the Known* is indeed a flawed book. But the handful of readers who took the time to hack through the technical and rhetorical brambles broke through to a sunlit clearing.

Sidney Ratner, who knew Dewey and Bentley and participated in their collaboration, argued that *Knowing and the Known* is not merely an authentic culmination of Dewey's thought, but a groundbreaking work in its own right. Its seminal concept, transaction, is systematic—not as a quest for ultimate truths but for seeing things in system: a systematic approach to analysis as experimental, contextual, and revisable rather than final and absolute.

Economist E. C. Harwood, founder of the American Institute for Economic Research, and his collaborator Rollo Handy, admired the book's experimental flexibility and its distaste for *a priori* theorizing and presumptuous central planning. They welcomed the systemic account of sign-behavior as scientifically superior to the then-fuzzy swagger of much writing in philosophy and economics.

In fact if not in name, today the transactional approach is dominant in the physical sciences and gaining ground in biological and behavioral fields such as anthropology, psychology, and even economics. However, it has not yet had a significant impact on our efforts to understand human nature in terms of a general theory of meaning and communication. Here interactional theories about mind and world still dominate, and holistic or ecological alternatives remain vague, poorly reasoned, or tinged with New Age mysticism. This book explores the down-to-earth transactional approach of Dewey and Bentley in hopes of finding some firm footing amid these shifting holistic sands.

2

The Challenge of Sense and Intellect

Philosophers delight in asking weird questions. Recently, I invited my class to respond to a two-part query: What one thing would you most like to know? Why is it important to know this? One student wrote "women," another "the last episode of *Lost,*" but most were sincere, with responses ranging from speculations about God to eliminating poverty. After some discussion, one student asked me how I'd reply. I pointed across the room and said, "I'd like to know that's actually a door, because if I can't be sure about the simplest things what chance do I have with these tougher questions?"

The class seemed a bit deflated by my answer, but this is typical of how philosophers go about their business. Philosophy has both a *way* of asking questions and a *what* that organizes them by content or subject-matter. The way, or method of philosophy, is implicit in the two parts of my question: I wanted the students to construct a simple argument— where one or more premises justify or support a conclusion. Philosophers are unimpressed by mere claims or assertions, no matter how obvious or heartfelt. Instead, the argument is the coin of the realm. An argument is good when true premises actually justify the conclusion.

My question also targeted the initial what of philosophy: What is most significant or real, and can I know this with certainty? The study of reality or being—of what is essential to the natural and human world—is called metaphysics. The nature of knowledge, truth, and certainty falls under epistemology. These culminate in a third, distinctly ethical question: What should I *do* about what I determine to be real and significant? What obligations, if any, does this knowledge impose upon actions involving myself and others?

What is real? What can I know? What should I do about it? This sequence of questions marks the metaphysical, epistemological, and ethical *what* of philosophical inquiry targeted by the *how* of reasoned arguments.

RATIONALISM AND EMPIRICISM

Philosophy also involves a perspective or point of view. Ogden Nash once said that nobody agrees with anybody else, but adults hide their disagreements better than babies. If so, then philosophers are quintessential *l'enfants terribles*! Still, in all the quibbling among creeds, cliques, and cabals, two prevalent cross currents extend back to the origins of Western philosophy in ancient Greece some 2,500 years ago. These crosscurrents, *rationalism* and *empiricism*, celebrate our dual propensity for idealistic visions and hard-nosed facts. Over the centuries they drifted apart, creating an adversarial gap that has discredited philosophy and hindered science—a gap Dewey and Bentley committed their careers to closing.

In deciding what is ultimately real and how we can know it, rationalists emphasize intellect over what we perceive by way of our senses. From their perspective we "see" more clearly with our minds than with our eyes, thus knowing what is real or true is a matter of proper reasoning rather than perceiving. Rationalism's central tenet is, "Objects conform to mind."

The opposing current, empiricism, puts sense experience before intellect. Empiricists claim we know the real world most directly by looking or pointing at things rather than thinking about them—*that* yellow notepad, *that* door, *that* cat. Reason and analysis are important, but they can only work on perceptual content *given* to us from real things in the physical, mind-independent world. Empiricism's creed, accordingly, is "Mind conforms to objects."

PLATO'S BIG IDEAS

One of the first great rationalists, Plato (427 B.C.-347 B.C.), invites us to compare a triangle we can see and feel, perhaps draw on a blackboard or cast in iron, to the concept of triangle generated in thought: two nonparallel lines on a plane surface bisected by a third line.

Initially, we're inclined to say the physical construct is the real triangle, while the definition is merely a thought or idea about it. But consider the situation carefully. The lines of the definition are perfectly straight, but no physical triangle has perfectly straight lines. The lines of a triangle have no width, but a physical triangle can't exist without lines of a certain width. A triangle is defined as having angles amounting to exactly 180°, but under magnification any drawn edge will look jagged, thus the sum of the angles of three such intersecting lines will never be exactly 180°. And where the definition of triangle remains the same regardless of time, no physical triangle—even one made of platinum—will last forever.

These considerations lead Plato to the unexpected conclusion that although any physical triangle is necessarily imperfect, the concept of triangle is eternally true and absolutely perfect. Still not convinced? Consider that the physical triangle depends upon the definition or idea, but not the reverse. Even if we had the magical power to destroy all the physical triangles in nature, "two nonparallel lines on a plane surface..." would still define "triangle." But a physical triangle that does not conform to the definition, in its imperfect way, is unthinkable.

According to Plato, what holds for triangles is true of everything. So, for example, the concept of cat is more real than any particular cat, and the concept of human is more real than any given person. True reality consists of a hierarchy of intellectual ideas, or *forms*; physical objects are inferior copies of these. Since ideas are more real than material objects, forms of things not burdened by physical bodies such as Truth, Justice, and Beauty are higher than forms of humans, cats or trees. The ultimate form—the culmination of Truth, Justice, and Beauty—is the Form of Good.

DESCARTES' DEMONIC DOUBTS

The great French philosopher René Descartes (1596-1650) advanced a modern form of rationalism. Like many intellectuals of his era, Descartes admired the pioneering science of Nicolaus Copernicus (1473-1543), Galileo Galilei (1564-1642), and Johannes Kepler (1571-1630). They determined that the celestial progression was neither the handiwork of an inner life force nor a guiding divine hand, but rather an expression of exact and universal mechanical laws. Descartes aspired to set philosophy on the same firm foundations as the physical sciences. Reasoning that he couldn't claim to know anything about which he wasn't absolutely certain, he devised a method of doubt to decide which of his beliefs was impervious to doubt. Employing this method, Descartes would have frowned upon my students' hopes to comprehend God or the causes of poverty—claims about such things are clearly doubtable. But so too are common sense assertions we'd normally never question, such that bread is nourishing or that the road I'm traveling will take me home.

Applied assiduously, Descartes' method leads to the shocking conclusion that almost everything is susceptible to doubt. In fact, how can I be completely sure I'm not now dreaming or that the external world—seemingly so solid and secure—is more than a phantasm? For all I really know, I might be under the hypnotic spell of a demonic evil genius bent upon deceiving me about the basic facts of my world, including the elementary truths of arithmetic and geometry. Perhaps I don't even have a body, but am a disembodied brain floating in a vat, stimulated to perceive a world that is really a program in the demon's supercomputer. I don't believe such a scenario, but how can I be absolutely sure it isn't so?

Despite this wholesale assault upon knowledge, Descartes found one statement impervious to doubt. Sure, it's T-shirt fodder these days: "I think, therefore I drink…I wink"—just insert a clever predicate. But that doesn't diminish the originality or brilliance of *cogito ergo sum:* "I think, therefore I am." The point is stunningly simple. I can doubt the existence of God, my own body, or even the external world itself. But I cannot doubt the existence of a doubter. The very ability to doubt implies that *I* exist to do the doubting.

With the cogito, Descartes has secured his foundation for knowledge and scientific philosophy. I know I am a "thinking thing" and that any consequence that clearly follows from this basic insight is also secure. From here we can build a strategy for restoring many of the beliefs we've come to doubt:

1. I know I exist and think, and my thoughts include ideas of perfection and infinity. But I'm imperfect and my powers are finite. Since no imperfect being can create perfection, I couldn't have made myself with these perfect ideas on my own. So I'm not alone in the world. There's also an unlimited being who created both me and these ideas of perfection I experience. I call this being God.

2. I've entertained the possibility of a deceitful demon who could trick me into perceiving things that aren't really there. But the God who created me and my ideas of perfection is necessarily also perfect. So besides being all knowing and all powerful, such a God must be all loving, all caring, and totally honest as well. Callousness or deceit, after all, would be evidence of imperfection.

3. Since God is loving, caring, and honest, he cannot be a demonic genius bent upon deceiving me about the nature of the external world.

4. Therefore, even though I experience only my own perceptions and mental states, and not the external world directly, God makes sure the world I sense is much like the world that actually exists.

If you find this argument appealing, you might just be a rationalist. Even if you don't, you have to admire its chutzpah. The upshot of Descartes' demonstration is that I can know many things about myself and the external world, including knowledge of perceived objects, God, and mathematical relations. Though few philosophers accept Descartes' sinuous proof, many are attracted to the idea that reality is mind-based. Some, such as Baruch Spinoza (1632-1677) and Gottfried Leibniz (1646-1715), look beyond the individual cogito to the infinite power of God's mind, of which the world itself is a manifestation. Others suggest that reality is most fully and authentically disclosed in the mathematical physics championed by Newton and his successors. These reflect different eddies in the river of rationalism—the belief that objects conform to mind.

MAKING THINGS OF SENSE

Rationalism's counterweight, empiricism, holds that the real world is physical and given to us by way of our senses. Like rationalism, empiricism also traces its lineage back to ancient Greece. The first Western philosopher, Thales (624 B.C.-546 B.C.), was a materialist who believed all reality consists of various densities of water. A later refinement, atomism, speculated that differences among various solids, liquids, and gases are actually different combinations of uniform microscopic particles, a view remarkably prescient of contemporary molecular physics and chemistry.

The father of modern scientific empiricism, John Locke (1632-1704), agreed with Descartes that we directly experience only perceptions of things and not the external realities themselves. But Locke denied that this has to be coordinated by God or grasped by some intellectual insight. In fact, he argued, starting with the mind in order to determine how objects are derivative of it is a completely backward approach. Even 17th-century science was advanced enough to realize that external realities stimulate our sense organs in ways that create mental replicants in our minds. A competent theory of knowledge, accordingly, should focus on how an object causes a perceptual experience as its effect. Figure 1 on page 12 illustrates the empiricist model where mind conforms to objects.

A key claim of the empiricist theory of knowledge, atomism, is that we do not have a sense impression of, say, a complete cube. Instead, Locke held that we have multiple "simple" impressions of white, off-white, and figures denoting a square and two polygons. Locke's great successor, David Hume

11

Figure 1. **The Empiricist Model of Perception**

Empiricists claim we perceive the external world indirectly (represented by the figure on the left), through mental sense impressions or appearances caused by external physical things (figure on the right).

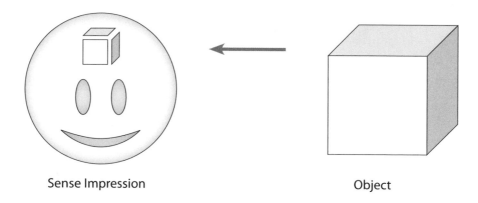

Sense Impression   Object

(1711-1776), surmised that we make faint copies of these impressions, *simple ideas,* we subsequently preserve in memory. It is our ability to retrieve and associate simple ideas that allows us to "bundle" them into discrete objects, called *complex ideas,* and also to construct general terms or concepts. The recurrent combination of certain colors and figures, for example, builds up the complex idea of *that* cube. Then the experience of different cubes forms the *general idea* of cube that is its concept or definition. This atomistic assembly line extends all the way from mundane things like cubes and cats to the laws of nature themselves. Even Newton's laws of motion are not the immutable handwriting of God or necessity. Instead, they are patterns assembled from observation of particulars along with the expectation, though by no means the assurance, that they will continue in the future.

This reveals another point of contention between rationalism and empiricism. For rationalists, only general ideas and their inferences are certain; perceptual experiences are often false or deceptive. Empiricists, to the contrary, hold that sense impressions and simple ideas are the assured givens we generalize into less certain regularities and laws. Both rationalism and empiricism aspire to an absolutely firm foundation for knowledge, a quest for certainty, though in opposite directions. Is one alternative right, or is there a pox on both houses requiring a new approach? The judgment of history leans toward the pox.

GENIE'S REVENGE: THE SKEPTICAL CHALLENGE

However skillfully they defended their own positions, empiricists and rationalists were even more talented at undermining each other. Empiricists derided the utopian metaphysics of their rivals: Truly scientific philosophy doesn't just manipulate concepts; it digs into things, scrapping and clawing for nature's secrets. In their turn, rationalists noted that no mere tallying of empirical events, such as dropping rocks to illustrate gravity, explains the universality of scientific laws. But their trump card was empiricism's entanglement in the problem of the external world, a skeptical challenge that to this day remains the most obdurate problem of epistemology and perhaps of philosophy itself.

The skeptical challenge, in a nutshell, focuses upon the seemingly unbridgeable gap between experienced appearances and the real external existences that purportedly cause or underlie them. If we perceive the world indirectly, by means of appearances or sense impressions, how can we possibly get outside of these to see how the world really is? Imagine living our entire lives in a windowless room, with only a television monitor to inform us about the external world. If these images and sounds are faithful copies of what's really there, then there's no problem about knowing the world: Knowledge, though indirect, faithfully replicates what's actually out there. But, smiles the skeptic, how do we know these appearances are faithful copies? We can't get around the monitor, or ourselves, even once, to check and see. So the mere appearances, no matter how reliable they seem to be, don't even constitute evidence from which we can say our knowledge of the world is probable or likely. For all we know or have any right to believe, Descartes' demonic genius may be controlling the transmission.

KANT'S COPERNICAN REVOLUTION

No sane person, of course, actually believes the experienced world is a grand illusion, and to conventional wisdom such skeptical talk merely confirms the silliness of philosophy. Underlying such silliness, however, are serious questions about evidence, knowledge, and common-sense notions about the world and how we perceive it.

Many believe the first constructive answers came from the great German philosopher Immanuel Kant (1724-1804). Surmising that both empiricism and rationalism were incomplete, each overlooking important insights from the other, Kant orchestrated a grand synthesis he called transcendental idealism. Empiricism rightly holds that evidence of the senses is vital to understanding the world.

But rationalism, he said, is correct on two counts. First, universal principles of reason overlie sensed particulars, and these explain the general applicability of scientific laws. Second, objects conform to mind: What we recognize and work with are not copies of mind-independent realities. Instead they reflect our unique human capacity for making sense of things by making things out of sense!

Kant called this twist a new Copernican Revolution. Copernicus had ascertained that the earth is not a fixed center from which all external planetary movement is determined. The earth, instead, revolves around the sun and planetary motion is determined relative to the motion of earthbound observers. Kant, in a similar vein, argues philosophically that an external object is not a fixed and complete reality that simply gives itself to the human mind, as our diagram of empiricism supposes. Instead, we can't help but see things relative to abilities we possess as human observers, and it is in this way that objects conform to mind.

An attentive reader might suspect an ambiguity here. Is Kant saying that external objects *are* purely constructs of the mind? Or is he saying that although external things have their own properties and characteristics, *we* only experience uniquely human derivatives? On its face, either choice looks bad for Kant. The first smacks of extreme rationalism, except instead of God, each of us makes our world. The second resuscitates empiricism, but with no hope of knowing things as they are in-themselves.

That Kant is offering a genuine middle way between rationalism and empiricism, and not merely peddling an ambiguity, requires a deeper understanding of his claim that objects conform to mind. First, and of utmost importance, we must realize that Kant's *mind* is not the empiricist notion of brain functions operating "between the ears." After all, so far as ears and brains are objects, they are just as external to our experienced appearances as cubes or doors. So, at least for the moment, we must stop thinking like empiricists: instead of an object of some kind, let's think about the mind as a function.

Whereas an object is a discrete thing, a function is about how something is done. As a function, "mind" means roughly "What do you have *in mind*? What do you need to do, resolve, or figure out?" Everyone agrees that objects are experienced. For Kant, mind consists of the conditions of such experiences— what we must be able to do in order to have an experience of an object. There are two such general conditions, *sense* and *intellect,* that respectively reflect the strengths of empiricism and rationalism within Kant's synthesis.

The components of sense are *space* and *time.* Space is not, as we commonly

Figure 2. **Kant's Transcendental Idealism**

For Kant, mind is not a physical brain, but the sum of conditions necessary to experience an object. The convergence of arrows above shows how sense and intellect together produce our experience of an object.

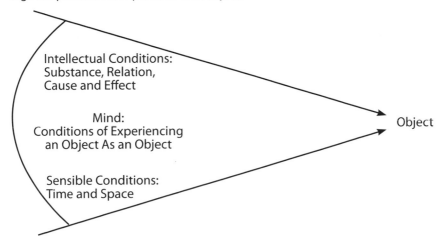

suppose, the "box out there" in which things-in-themselves exist, nor is time the fluid "something" that flows from past to future within such a box. Upon empiricist assumptions, both the "box" and the "flowing" would be unreachable from mere appearances. Instead, space and time are conditions of mind in which the raw materials of perception are organized into coherent objects. Stated negatively, we can't experience an object as an object unless we experience it *in space* and *in time*. Let's revisit the cube. If the cube didn't take up space, we couldn't experience it as a cube. If time were frozen, so too would be our sense-organs. Time and space, then, are conditions of experiencing an object as an object.

Reflecting rationalism's contribution are 12 intellectual conditions or categories Kant borrows from Aristotle, three of which are substance, relation, and cause and effect. Like time and space, categories are functional conditions of experience rather than objects or occult powers. *Substance* isn't some cosmic stuff underlying reality, but only the realization that any object must be substantial if we are to experience it—it must have content in time and space. Relation is the ability to distinguish what the object is from what it is not. If we couldn't discern the border or limit separating "this" from "not this," we couldn't experience discrete objects.

Finally, the ability to grasp what happens in the world in terms of cause and effect keeps everything from appearing random and chaotic. Without this ability, we couldn't make sense of the everyday world, let alone the scientific endeavor to find universal laws of nature. Since both common sense and science are possible, cause and effect must be a condition of experienced objects.

Figure 2 on page 15 indicates how objects are products of the synthesis of sense and intellect. These are real objects "out there" in the world, not constructs of sense impressions. There are, of course, brains and brain processes, but these too are objects that conform to the conditions of mind even as they provide us with a scientific account of perception and cognition.

HEGEL'S RESTLESS SPIRIT

While lauding Kant's synthesis, his successors found it flawed and still vulnerable to skepticism. Consider those little lines jutting from the top and bottom of the diagram. They look harmless, but what do they signify? If the top line indicates intellectual content beyond anything we can sense, what could this be?—Logical or mathematical axioms? Platonic forms? The Mind of God? If the bottom line points to sensory content beyond anything we can experience or even think about, aren't we right back in the skeptic's doghouse? Aren't we forced to accept mind-independent realities that feed raw data we assemble into experienced things, yet completely inaccessible to us as they really are?

Such concerns led later idealists, led by Georg Wilhelm Fiedrich Hegel (1770-1831), to regard sense and intellect as points of dialectical conflict within an integral unity. Instead of separate wellsprings merely brought together, he saw sense and intellect as opposite sides of the same coin—one side is the real world as we experience it, the other is what this world reveals about us as experiencers of it. Hegel, perhaps misleadingly, called this the progression of *self-consciousness,* though this actually means the interdependent unfolding of self and world. He also disagreed with Kant's static synthesis that merely places sense percepts under intellectual concepts. Instead, as indicated in Figure 3 on page 17, each new step begins with a dialectical conflict—a problem that negates what is currently accepted as knowledge and propels us toward something better and more comprehensive.

Hegel further dropped Kant's *a priori* categories of knowledge for conditions that evolve historically. We can trace this historical development by following the spiral from the inside out. The point of origination signifies an epoch when intellect was "sunken" in sense, when human cognition and self-awareness had not yet emerged from animal feelings and impulses. According to Hegel, the story of civilization is the gradual and hard-fought emergence of intellect from sense. The expanding spiral illustrates this gradual emergence of

Figure 3. **Hegel's Dialectic of Self-Consciousness**

Hegel sees history as the gradual freeing of intellect from sense. The interior of the spiral marks an initial state where beings are not yet self-aware. The widening spiral represents the ongoing emergence of intellect from sense still rooted in conflict.

| Conflict/Negation

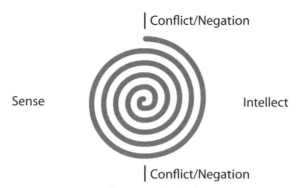

Sense   Intellect

| Conflict/Negation

individual and social awareness coincident with an enhanced understanding of the natural and empirical world. Each achieved advance, each "Eureka, I've found it!" is inevitably checked by a new problem or challenge we fight through to yet another level of understanding.

There is much speculation as to whether Hegel thought this dialectical progression, this sojourn of Spirit, has a final victorious outcome—a final conquest of sense by intellect. Hegel himself speaks of the aspirations of the *Absolute*, and some Christian interpreters saw this as a philosophically abstruse allusion to the Judgment Day: the reunion of worthy human souls with God's eternal intellect and the dissolution of the physical world. Others, such as Karl Marx, regarded the Absolute as the triumph of human reason over selfish and debased material greed: the dawn of a utopian worker's paradise.

But a third, transactional, possibility, is that Hegel's Absolute is really just the spiral itself—an open-ended series of challenges and conquests that has no final denouement unless we manage to obliterate ourselves along the way. On this view the very notion of paradise, supernatural or social, is repugnant to our nature. Challenge, conquest, new challenge—this is the rhythm of human life. This is what we are. We're home in such a world, neither free-wheeling intellects bent upon overcoming sense, nor sense-confined creatures lamenting the loss of the real world. The world makes us, and we remake the world. Progress can be measured from one loop of the spiral to the next, but never finally or absolutely. In Hegel's contorted phrase, in negating itself the Absolute makes itself possible.

3

Dewey's Circuit of Inquiry

Even as a young student at the University of Vermont, Dewey sensed that his life's goal was to overcome the divisions of heaven and hell, spirit and matter, saved and damned—a mission impressed upon him by New England Calvinism. He was naturally attracted to Hegel, whose integration of intellect and sense promised not only to mend the philosophical rifts of subject and object, self and world, but also to deliver the divine into the realm of human dreams and aspirations. Later acknowledging the "permanent deposit" Hegel left in his thought, Dewey searched for an organic unity that would eradicate mind-independent reality once and for all. Like Kant, Dewey sought a functional solution to the rift between empiricism and rationalism. But his functionalism ran deeper than Kant's. It is not simply sense placed under concepts, but sense as evidence for resolving encountered problems that is vital to objective knowledge. Dewey agrees with Kant that objects conform to mind, but mind is more than a set of conditions of knowledge. Instead, mind is a dynamic function of "minding" or successfully managing problems.

SURVIVAL IS A FITNESS

By the turn of the century, Dewey's idealism had fully matured into pragmatism and naturalism. He preferred Darwin's theory of evolution, where self-consciousness is a tool for adapting to environmental changes, to the inexorable triumph of the Hegelian Absolute in a Christian heaven or a workers' paradise. But he equally shunned the simplistic "red in tooth and claw" view of evolution. For Dewey, survival of the fittest means more than the dominion of the strongest, greediest, or most cunning individuals. Instead, of greater importance is the fit of organisms within their environment: how well they adapt themselves to their surroundings and vice versa. As such, the book of nature is not primarily a story about the struggle for power, but of the ongoing co-adaptation of organisms and environments involving cooperation as well as competition. Human intelligence is as much an evolutionary product as fangs and feathers, though it provides its bearers with the singular advantage of greater control over encountered problems.

HABIT AND DOUBT-BELIEF

For Dewey, problem-solving activity is the common method we employ for any understanding of objects and objectivity. But he rejects foundationalism—the belief that certain privileged or given bits of knowledge underlie everything else we can know. Though they disagree about its content, both rationalists and empiricists still seek such basic knowledge as the brass ring of philosophy. Rationalists look for logical certitude or self-evident truths; empiricists hope their sense percepts replicate some feature of the corresponding physical world. But, warns Dewey, either version of this purported "knowledge relation" inevitably divides what we can conceive or perceive from what is truly real. Rationalists admit the frailness of our cognitive faculties compared to God's omniscient mind. Empiricists concede the unbridgeable gap between mental appearances and mind-independent reality.

Dewey is not antagonistic toward knowledge, and he agrees that grasping the relation between what is known and how we know it is very much the point of science and common sense alike. What bothers Dewey—indeed, bothers him enough to call it "the philosophers' fallacy"—is the careless assumption that some idea or theory that is actually the reflective outcome of an analysis of experience must be there at the beginning. Should the need arise I could experience my bookshelf as a set of colored patches. But does this mean I typically begin with a set of discrete patches that I subsequently assemble into books? If not, then any theory that insists that such simple ideas are the building blocks of all perception commits the philosophers' fallacy. Dewey hoped for a better empiricism, an immediate empiricism more faithful to experience in everyday life.

Until the middle of the 19th century, philosophy and psychology tended to regard human cognition as essentially reflective. It likened human consciousness to a lighthouse beacon continually illuminating its surrounding terrain, bringing all it touched into a knowledge relation. Habit was considered an inferior faculty—a set of animal instincts humans transcend by means of

Figure 4. **Peirce's Circle of Doubt-Belief**

According to Peirce, we think primarily to get ourselves out of trouble. The circle below traces the process through which a habituated belief is challenged by doubt and inquiry leads to a satisfactory answer. This solution becomes part of a renewed background of habits.

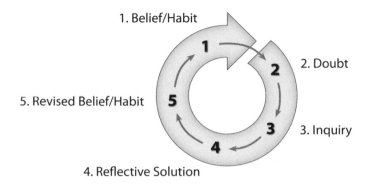

1. Belief/Habit

2. Doubt

5. Revised Belief/Habit

3. Inquiry

4. Reflective Solution

refined reflection. Though anticipated by Aristotle and Hume, the great psychologist-philosopher William James (1842-1910) first popularized the alternative that habit dominates our everyday preoccupations, thus the default mode of experience is more nonreflective than reflective. Even before James, Charles S. Peirce (1839-1914) suggested that these habituated beliefs are the mainstay of experience. We think primarily for the limited purpose of getting ourselves out of trouble—that is, when our habits find themselves conflicted or challenged by doubt.

Such considerations make it clear that habits are not merely instincts. Instead, they are predispositions to behave in certain ways that accumulate over a lifetime of experiences. We couldn't function without habituated beliefs— we take our next breath without wondering whether it is poison gas, sit on chairs we assume will support our weight, drive through green signal lights confident that side traffic will stop. It is only when such expectations are disrupted by an unexpected problem—the air has a strange odor, the chair begins to wobble, the traffic light is out—that Peirce finds us cast into doubt and compelled to do something about it. Even here, habit itself may supply a ready solution—say, grab another chair—which cuts off the need to think. As shown in Figure 4 on page 21, it is a problem that sticks—that produces sustained doubt—that calls forth cognitive inquiry in order to determine what is wrong and what we should do about it. Once a solution is achieved, thought has served its purpose and a state of habituated belief is restored. It is not the original belief, however, but belief informed by what we have learned through the function of inquiry.

Peirce and James pioneered what is now called classical American pragmatism, whose motto is "Knowing is doing." Pragmatism follows Kant and Hegel in reconciling empiricism and rationalism, yet surpasses both in accounting for the integration of sense and intellect. Experience dominated by habit is, as Hegel suggests, "sunken in sense" with no differentiation of subject and object. Yet this is sense informed by previous reflective solutions. Because I've learned how to write, I pay no attention to the pen I'm using or to myself as its user. On the other hand, sense equally informs intellect in that acquired habits help us recognize problems as problems: A small sound unnoticed by the average motorist signifies both an engine problem to the trained mechanic and a clue to thinking about how to repair it. In pragmatism, Hegel's quest for the unity of sense and intellect—his tortured "possibility of the absolute in its own self-negation"—becomes the interplay of habit and thought in problem-solving activities working to establish stable beliefs.

NONREFLECTIVE EXPERIENCE

Dewey joins Peirce and James in insisting that philosophy attend to nonreflective experience as well as reflective experience, a distinction he calls "having" versus "knowing." Dewey utilizes the having-knowing distinction to take aim at the kingpin of philosophical "seeing apart"—the problem of the external world. His solution is simple yet profound. Both rationalists and empiricists get off track by setting things up as the problem of how my mind presumably gets to external realities beyond itself. But this is not what is experienced! Instead, in its default or nonreflective mode experience does not distinguish an "in here" from an "out there," a "myself" set against an "other." Instead, Dewey finds nonreflective experience to be an "integral unity" of both.

To make sense of this, let's try a little pragmatic experiment. Consider the status of the letter…

"g"

…in the word "integral" above. This "g" has, of course, a clearly demarked set of properties—it is black, consists of a seraphed circle above an oval, and is the seventh letter of the alphabet. It is reflectively experienced as having these qualities now, because I've drawn your attention to it. I've made it the problem.

But here's the key question. What was the experience of this "g" just before this happened? At the end of that paragraph, the focal problem was the meaning of "integral unity." Obviously the "g" was there; it was part of the total sense content available to you. But my guess is that you didn't experience it as a distinct mark. Long ago you mastered the alphabet and basic rules of grammar.

In conforming to these habituated expectations, the "g" was part of an "integral unity"—the nonreflective background of experience characterized not by discrete properties such as black or ovals, but by a fit that "hangs together" as a gestalt or a unity. In Dewey's phrase, it was "had" but not discretely "known". It is only when this habituated background is disrupted by something unexpected or problematic—encountering "inteGral," "intergal," or having your attention drawn to it—that the "g" stands forth and becomes a subject of reflective focus.

Dewey thinks this discovery about experience can be generalized. Consider, for example, the book or screen that holds these words. It, too, is a tangible thing with discrete properties. But, again, I'll bet it wasn't reflectively isolated as a book or screen prior to my mentioning it just now. It, too, was "had" within the perceptual whole, but not reflectively "known."

In fact, let's raise the stakes by throwing in the priciest chip—were you consciously thinking of yourself set apart from the these words as a discrete and separate reader? If not, perhaps it's a mistake to presume that a philosophical understanding of objectivity starts by asking how an individual mind gets to mind-independent reality. Perhaps this commits the philosophers' fallacy of allowing some supposition or theory to obscure accepting things as they're actually experienced.

RETHINKING REALITY

Traditional empiricism claims we know the external world indirectly, by means of sense perceptions or appearances. As we've seen, this invites the skeptical challenge—the dismal conclusion that there's no way to get around these appearances to experience the world as it really is. But rather than conceding this as the unavoidable scourge of philosophy, or frantically searching for a miraculous way to defeat it, external world skepticism might be a helpful warning to us that this basic approach is misguided, with an invitation to rethink our fundamental ideas about the world and our place in it. Dewey welcomes this invitation. To confront core questions of knowledge and reality in a way faithful to things as they are actually experienced, Dewey introduces his *postulate of immediate empiricism*:

What *is* is what it is experienced *as*.

Eight little words. So simple. So enigmatic! What is Dewey saying? If the postulate makes sense at all, at first it sounds a little nutty. If things become real just by experiencing them, let's get rich quick by imagining extra digits in our account balances! Clearly we don't create realities just by thinking about them, and we're also inundated with experiences that are not what they seem to be: miracle diets, investment schemes, politicians' promises—not to mention dreams, hallucinations, and good old-fashioned mistakes. Clearly Dewey isn't counseling wholesale gullibility, obstinacy, or insanity. So what is he suggesting?

Dewey is trying to get philosophers, and those who read them, to stop fussing about what is and isn't real. He's not making the ludicrous claim that we create the world by our experiences, but only the obvious point that whatever we experience really is experienced that way. If philosophy starts with a creditable analysis of experience, and if every experience really is that experience, including even dreams and errors, then nothing philosophically significant hangs on the question of reality.

To see Dewey's point, imagine being alone in a cabin in the woods, absorbed in a suspenseful novel. I don't experience myself reading the book—it's the story that's alive, the intrigue of the characters in the plot. Suddenly the reverie is broken by a *TAP! TAP! TAP!* What is *that*? An intruder? *I* put the *book* down. *I* investigate my idea. Shortly I discover that, no, it's merely a shade tapping in a newly risen wind. I return to my book, and within moments am again wrapped up in the story. The shade taps intermittently, but it's barely noticed. After awhile, it's not noticed at all.

In this account, the play of reflective and nonreflective experience affects the very way we think about reality. Lost in the narrative, neither the book, myself, nor the contents of the surrounding room stand out as reflective objects—they are "had" rather than "known." They really are experienced that way, and that's what they really are in such experience. But the unexpected sound marks an abrupt onset of doubt; it triggers an experience of fright-at-the-sound that really is experienced as frightful. In subsequent inquiry, *I* stand forth to investigate the discrete contents of the room, and ultimately conclude the sound really is a window shade tapping.

Discovery of the window shade is clearly more useful than the earlier experience of fright. It rectifies that experience, for there was no need to have been frightened. However, even though the reflective conclusion is more useful and comprehensive than the preceding experiences, it isn't more real. Both the nonreflective unity and the fright really were experienced as such.

Dewey's goal is to eradicate the obtuse and skeptic-baiting problem of how mental appearances get to mind-independent realities. In its stead, he's promoting a correlation between what poses itself as a problem or challenge to inquiry and what provides a useful or satisfactory resolution. That subjects and objects emerge as respondents to problem-solving situations seems more faithful to actual experience than sense impressions or demonic geniuses. So long as nonreflective having dominates, self and object are not discretely segregated. These are discriminated instead, in response to an encountered problem, where *I* stand forth to propose the idea for resolving it.

The goal of such a proposal is to achieve an "objective" that resolves the disruption—a plan of action that results in the determination that "Oh, it was just a window shade tapping." Mind is not the subjective realm of appearances locked up inside the head, but the function of "minding" or managing problems. An object is not some inaccessible mind-independent reality, but the attained "objective" of such directed activity

PLURALISM AND THE HOW OF OBJECTIVITY

We may well imagine a critic's incredulous reaction. Am I suggesting that neither I nor the objects in the room existed before the disruption? Did I just pop into being in response to the problem, together with the discrete contents of the external world? Of course not, but to explain this takes two steps. First, notice that the problem of "what was there all along" in response to a philosophical challenge is a different problem—a different experience—than the situation experienced in the cabin. The philosophical problem is not to account for a potential threat, but to specify what sorts of things have continued existence, all things considered. This problem invites a different inquiry—one in which I am justified, in fact obligated, to stand forth and state "I was there all along, and so was the room and its contents."

In terms of reality, this illustrates pragmatism's commitment to pluralism: With different problems in different contexts, there are different "reals" to be experienced and reported. In the traditional view, there is one ultimate in-itself reality, known only when it corresponds to a privileged appearance. But once we see that this both invites the skeptical challenge and has no basis in actual experience, we are open to the suggestion that there may be as many reals as there are solutions to inquiries that arise in a limitless variety of contexts. Dewey claims, for instance, there is no in-itself horse beyond or behind its various uses and enjoyments: it really is an investment for its owner, a safe rider for a purchaser with children, and an anatomical specimen for an equine physiologist. If we tend to see the "real horse" in terms of some standard definition or scientific account, it is because such concepts have an especially rich variety of connected applications, not because they approach some philosophical fiction called in-itself reality.

Here's the second step. Kant's appeal to function, we recall, was not to catalog what makes up the universe, but to explain how the experience of objectivity is possible. As a general theory of reality and knowledge, this is also the aim of pragmatism. What there is in the world is vitally important, of course, but that's a matter of empirical exploration, not philosophical speculation. As a philosophical function or method, transactional pragmatism is charged with showing how anything can be known—namely, as an attained objective of problem-solving activity. We do not begin with separate subjective minds and real external objects and try to figure out how one can reach out to or interact with the other. Instead, we start with an integral unity of nonreflective experience from which selves and objects emerge as phases of problem-solving activities. Given that they spark the drive to diagnose and resolve problems, doubt and uncertainty are essential to this function, but directionless doubt about mind-independent reality gains no traction in a transactional world.

THE CIRCUIT OF INQUIRY

Let's take a moment to review the argument for a transactional theory of knowledge and objectivity.

1. Since experience is our window to the world, attention to how things are actually experienced is vital to any account of knowledge and objectivity.
2. Neither rationalism's self-evident truths nor empiricism's sense-impressions faithfully capture the dynamic of actual experience. In different ways, they commit the philosopher's fallacy of supposing that the product of some reflective theory about experience initiates actual experience.
3. Attention to actual experience suggests that its default mode is nonreflective instead of reflective—dominated by habit rather than self-evident truths or brightly lit sense data. Perceptual content is not discretely

parceled into things and thoughts. It is an integral unity, a gestalt or fit that is had rather than known. The disruption of this unity by something unexpected or problematic initiates the cognitive distinction of thing and thought, self and other.

4. For rationalism, knowledge of reality consists of valid deductions from self-evident intuitions. Empiricism sees the knowledge relation as a correspondence between a privileged appearance and an in-itself reality. Dewey's postulate of immediate empiricism—What *is* is what it is experienced *as*—undercuts both self-evident and correspondent views of reality. Faithful to actual experience, "real" merely admits the obvious fact that whatever is experienced really is experienced that way. Although reflectively discerned objects may be more useful or informative than the initial gestalt or transitional shock, they are not more real.

5. Two consequences follow from this:

   A. Philosophical pluralism. There are as many "reals" as the unlimited number of problems, inquiries, and achieved solutions through which these may be "realized."

   B. Transaction as *function*. Philosophy's first task is to determine *how* objectives are projected and realized. What is real or objective is never independent of how it may be realized as an outcome of problem-solving activity.

Even though he never quite managed to assemble them systematically, Dewey worked on each of these steps in 26 years of teaching and research at Columbia University, a period that cemented his reputation as America's greatest philosopher. Of course, being a philosopher in the mid-20th century was nothing to brag about. The kerfuffle between rationalism and empiricism dragged on without resolution, and bright young minds turned to the physical and behavioral sciences to unlock the secrets of nature and the human mind. Remaining students of philosophy—positivists, postmodernists, deconstructionists—tallied excuses for putting themselves out of business.

Though enthusiastic about science and painfully aware of philosophy's woes, Dewey hoped to reconstruct philosophy rather than abet its demise. No spectrograph or litmus test can resolve our broad and enduring questions about existence, objectivity, knowledge, and value. Headway in such matters suggests, instead, an honest and sustained inquiry into experience as the first step toward building a worldview Dewey and Bentley would ultimately call transaction.

Figure 5. **Dewey's Circuit of Inquiry**

With Dewey, nonreflective experience (left) is disrupted by a problem that stimulates inquiry. We solve that problem by testing a hypothesis through the use of physical tools and data. This experiment leads to the realized object, which returns to and enriches the nonreflective background.

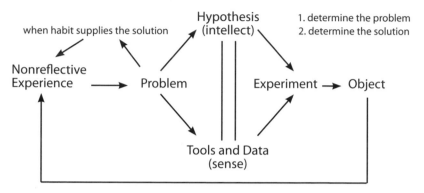

Dewey retired from active teaching in 1930, intending not, as might be supposed, to pursue the gentler life of the lecture circuit or golf course, but to "really get some work done." The urgency to bring together the scattered facets of his theory of experience eventually overcame his aversion to systematic thinking. The fruit of a decade-long effort, *Logic: The Theory of Inquiry* (1938) was widely praised and largely neglected. Logicians dismissed it because of its dearth of symbols and formal deductions—their understanding of scientific logic. They weren't open to the suggestion that a compendium of formal relations is merely one piece in a puzzle that connects reason to problem-solving activity.

Perhaps the highlight of the *Logic* is the "pattern of inquiry," where Dewey finally unites the diverse pieces of his theory of knowledge and objectivity. The default mode of getting along when all seems well with our world remains the undifferentiated unity of nonreflective habit. But life's first lesson is that things can, and often do, go wrong. This shock, this disruption of habit, marks the onset of a problematic situation—an initial cognitive awareness that something is wrong and something must be done about it. When the answer is easy and readily available, the return to nonreflective experience is quick and uneventful. But when the problem is obstinate, the solution not obvious, genuine inquiry is necessary. We need to devise a plan, idea, or hypothesis—first to diagnose the problem and then to decide how to resolve it.

Dewey's circuit of inquiry, sketched in Figure 5 on page 28, is a refinement of Peirce's circuit of belief-doubt and a capstone to Hegel's organic unity of intellect and sense. Reason is an indispensable human asset, but it is neither self-contained consciousness nor a spiritual force. Instead, it is essential for resolving problems. Our ability to think evolved as a "clutch" between a stimulus to action and an immediate physical response: a way to play out responses and their consequences in imagination before having to place our bodies at risk. But intellect does not operate in a vacuum. It requires physical instruments, tools, and data—often to diagnose a problem and formulate a hypothesis to resolve it, almost always when putting the hypothesis to the test.

Where Kant accepts a formal integration of intellect and sense and Hegel revels in dialectical tensions, Dewey insists upon experimentation, the actual testing of one's idea or plan. It is the encountered world, rather than the elegance of one's reasoning, that ultimately determines the worth of a hypothesis.

Once a hypothesis is experimentally confirmed, inquiry has achieved its objective or object. This is Dewey's ingenious solution to one of philosophy's most intractable problems. Plato, we recall, wondered how sensed particulars "copy" conceptual forms. Aristotle wanted to know how particular substances are shaped by essences. The doctors of the medieval church argued endlessly about how God's intellect "ingresses" upon matter to shape it according to his will. In modern times, beginning with Descartes, we tend to see either a radical separation of matter and mind or a reduction of one to the other. These days it's usually the latter—the identification of consciousness with physical neurological processes. Dewey's pluralism is fully open to physiological explanations when the problem is about the physical composition of an object, even one as complex as the human brain. To this sort of question, the best answer seems to be that consciousness really is a set of neurophysiological processes rather than some strange and immaterial mind-stuff.

But a philosophical understanding of objectivity is a different question answered by a different approach to reality. Here Dewey notes that an objective begins as a tentative idea or hypothesis proposed to resolve a problem. The successful testing of this idea results in its concrete physical realization. Quite literally the idea is "real-ized" in the object—not in any occult or metaphysical way, but in the relation of hypothesis to objective in experimental inquiry.

Much to the consternation of those who equate objects with mind-independent realities, Dewey's playful turn on "object" and "objective" is deliberate.

Aware of the dilemma inherent in trying to get from sense impressions to things-in-themselves, Dewey affirms Kant's Copernican Revolution—objects do conform to mind. Yet Dewey is even more insistent than Kant and Hegel that "mind" is not something subjective or simply "between the ears." Instead, "mind" signifies "minding" in the sense of directing available resources to the attentive management of problems, akin to "minding the store." Objects, accordingly, are products of constructive problem-solving activities—the attained objectives of inquiry. At both the individual and cultural level, our world is one of ongoing discovery. The "stick" of the infant becomes the child's "pencil;" further inquiry discloses a "graphite cylinder" with a core of allotropic carbon. A physicist further specifies an alignment of carbon atoms and perhaps envisions quarks and quantum fields. No single disclosure is the real object, let alone the philosopher's phantasmic thing-in-itself. There are simply an open-ended number of potential reals suited to various purposes and contexts of use.

This holds for natural objects as well as man-made ones. Though it seems paradoxical at first, the more we invest in ideas that lead to our understanding of things, the less we tend to think of them anthropocentrically, as like or dependent upon us. Our forbearers, who relied upon analogy and simple induction, imagined that the stars were campfires in the sky. Today we realize they are similar to our sun, yet far more distant—fueled by a hydrogen-to-helium conversion our ancestors could not have imagined. Science, in general, expands our understanding of natural process taking place far beyond our reach and long before our existence.

The reciprocal dependence of ideas and objects permeates, in fact, the entire circuit of inquiry. Once a solution is attained, the need for cognitive reflection ends. This doesn't mean the solution is no longer there, it's just that we can use it without having to fret or think about it. Attained objectives of inquiry—cognitive objects reflectively known—return to and enrich nonreflective experience. They dig the trenches of habit, of the tried and true, that help us get by without the continuous intervention of reflection. When problems inevitably arise, these settled meanings also serve as the tools and data—the pencils, hammers, and stethoscopes—we use to test hypotheses and achieve reflective objects that renew the circle by forging new settled meanings. As such, our progressive understanding of the encountered world is rooted in ongoing circuits of inquiry rather than self-evident truths or a correspondence between appearances and things-in-themselves.

That Dewey grasped the co-determination of idea and thing, subject and object, mind and matter, was evident as early as 1896 in "The Reflex Arc Concept in Psychology." The point of this important essay is that the mechanical model of stimulus and response should be replaced with a full organic circuit demanding the reciprocal interplay of dispositions, plans, and actions. This circuit of inquiry, which crops up in bits and pieces throughout Dewey's earlier writings, finally found a systematic expression four decades later in the *Logic* of 1938. Among his unfinished business, however, was coining a word capable of shouting this novel approach to knowledge and objectivity in no uncertain terms, and a work to showcase it in a general theory of meaning and communication. In the 1940s, and with Bentley's assistance, Dewey rose to this final challenge with the word transaction in a work called *Knowing and the Known*.

4

Self-Action, Interaction, and Transaction

In 1945, at the height of his collaboration with Arthur Bentley, Dewey proclaims that "to the degree in which the transactional is put over, the battle is won." He had devoted 15 years to the *Logic* and its central concept that what anything is cannot be severed from how we come to know and work with it. Though Dewey was nearly 80 when he finished the *Logic* in 1938, he was still looking ahead in his reflection to Bentley that "it wasn't a bad job at the time, but I could do better now, largely through association with you and getting the courage to try to see my thing through without compromise."

The *Logic* had developed a theory of inquiry—the idea that reason is not essentially a compendium of static rules and their derivations, but about how humans solve problems. What Dewey wanted to see through without compromise was the full mutual interdependence of *knowings* with *knowns*—where the function of knowing or naming anything is inseparable from whatever can be known or named. This "seeing together" what other theories break apart into separate things, thoughts, and actions is the essence of transaction. Our first task is to distinguish it from earlier self-actional and interactional approaches.

SELF-ACTION

Humans have always longed to understand their world. Survival itself depends upon finding out how the world rewards or frustrates our meager attempts to control it. Neurophysiology tells us the human brain grasps complex events more readily by constructing stories and narratives than by processing large quantities of data, and our ancestors created elaborate myths to explain natural events. Sitting around their fires, they saw lights in the sky and imagined the return gaze of celestial neighbors. The sparks from their flints inspired thoughts of thunderbolts flung by angry gods. The Mayans worshiped the rain deity Chaack, who dispensed favor and punishment with a lightning axe. The Romans parlayed a handful of inherited Greek gods into an ungainly gaggle of domestic deities responsible for everything from curdling milk to firing the hearth. The medieval mind saw all things illuminated by an inner, self-actional power or essence. Living things are animated by a life force or *élan vital*; bread nourishes due to its nutritive essence; a sedative has a dormative power that induces sleep.

INTERACTION

Today we regard self-actional reasoning as quaint, yet tend to overlook the boldness of vision needed to surpass it. For 2000 years, no one challenged Aristotle's idea that a body sustains its motion because of some continuous internal push. Galileo, working with rolling balls on inclined planes, first noticed that the motion of a body involves a trade-off between acceleration and resistance: not an inner push, but the interaction of opposing forces he called inertia. Newton subsequently made this the first of three laws that laid the foundation for modern mechanics and the scientific revolution itself. The Newtonian universe replaced a colorful cast of goblins, spooks, and spirits with what Albert Einstein (1879-1955) described as "simple forces between unalterable particles." Heat is not the effluence of restless brownies, but energy generated in the collision of molecules. A lightning strike is not a burst of outrage from an angry god, but an exchange of electrons and positive ions between cloud and ground. Life itself is not a vital force, but the pirouette of four basic proteins encoded as DNA.

The ability to see things interacting transformed our understanding of ourselves and our world. In suggesting that all macroscopic objects consist of colliding microscopic "corpuscles," the 17th-century Irish physicist Robert Boyle inaugurated modern physics and chemistry. From this it was a short step to the startling conclusion, teased in the next century by the French physician Julien de La Mettrie, that humans themselves may be likened to machines with interchangeable parts.

Interaction reshaped commerce and industry. The guild system of the late Middle Ages prized the master craftsman, whose skills reflected decades of apprenticeship. With the industrial revolution, the single artisan gave way to the factory system where production is broken into distinct tasks suitable to workers with lesser skills.

Such advances incurred costs. Though fanciful, anyone could appreciate the engaging world of myth. The world of mathematical physics is fathomed by an elite few. If the mind is a machine, or perhaps a network of electrochemical circuits, what becomes of purpose or meaning in life? If we are programmed like a computer, what does "free will" amount to? Seeing the world as a set of interchangeable parts has practical ramifications as well. Goods were expensive in the guild system, but supply and demand remained stable. The factory assembly line created cycles of boom and bust. Workers swarmed to cities seeking newly created jobs. Cheap labor and mass production drove down the cost of goods, and owners cut wages to remain competitive. When workers could no longer afford these goods, businesses collapsed and mass unemployment ensued until the cycle began again.

TRANSACTION

Dewey and Bentley realize that interaction is not *the* answer to how things work, but *an* answer. It is a conceptual tool, and like any tool it is appropriate for some tasks but wrong for others. They invite us to consider a third way of looking at objects and events, a transactional approach. Where self-action regards each entity as possessing an internal motivating force and interaction focuses upon causal relations among self-sufficient individuals, transaction sees the individual forged within a set of relations. In simplest terms, say Dewey and Bentley, transaction is "the right to see together…much that is talked about conventionally as if it were composed of irreconcilable separates." Where self-action and interaction look at a whole as the sum of its parts, transaction sees the parts as determined by the whole.

Transactional relations abound in everyday language. For example, "buyer" and "seller" are transactionally reciprocal—"buyer" is meaningless except in relation to "seller" and each seller must have at least a prospective buyer. Other codependent relations include "above-below," "hot-cold," "food-digestion," and "parent-child." Some transactions include three or more participants: "Hypotenuse" is the side of a triangle opposite the right angle formed by its other two sides; an "arbitrator" is a third party who settles a dispute between two litigants. Other transactional relations are open-ended, e.g. "citizen-government," "writer-reader," "one-whole number."

Even though Dewey and Bentley didn't consistently use the word "transaction" until the 1940s, the concept had been in development for decades. Transaction assumes an entire organism-environment system, rather than organisms acting in an external environment. Unlike the empiricism of separate sense impressions and external realities, it "sees together" mind and object as joint contributors to problem-solving activity. A hypothesis in inquiry has an object "in mind," and an attained object incorporates this idea within it.

SMALL TALK

No one denies that transactions have linguistic and social significance. The philosophical dispute concerns what is real in such cases. It's no coincidence that interaction became the paradigm of scientific explanation just as philosophy grew flush with empiricism, for the two go hand in hand. After all, most empiricists take the existence of mind-independent realities for granted. Things and their properties really are out there even if no one ever happens to experience them. Perceivers come to know these realities by interacting with them, but they certainly aren't created in perception. Even if nestled in some never explored cranny of the Kuiper belt beyond Pluto, they exist just as they are even if no one ever observes them.

Empiricism has the unenviable task of trying to get beyond perceived appearances to mind-independent realities. But, for the moment, let's put the problem of the external world aside. Even supposing an object is right there in front of us, fully and directly accessible, we face another obstacle to determining what it really and truly is. I declare it's a red door, and everyone else agrees with me—everyone, that is, except a traditional empiricist, a carpenter, and a physicist. The empiricist begins by reminding us that we really know only things as they are conveyed to our senses. I perceive only a red patch, a rectangle, and perhaps sensations associated with hearing and touching. To assemble these into a "door" involves a mental act beyond what is perceived in the data itself. The carpenter scoffs at the thought of being mesmerized by colors and sounds. A door is made out of panels, staves, stiles, rails, and also hinges, handles, and stops. The physicist trumps them both by declaring that the door is actually mostly empty space, sparsely populated by atoms of carbon, oxygen, and hydrogen assembled into molecules of cellulose and lignin. The physical realm really consists of such quanta. Though colors, sounds, and macroscopic objects are useful fictions that help us make sense of our world, they do not actually exist.

The belief that ordinary objects really consist of constituent particles and the forces that bind them is called *reductionism*. Among its many champions was the famous British philosopher Bertrand Russell (1872-1970), who felt physicists alone are qualified to explore the secrets of ultimate reality, and that scientifically-minded philosophers should defer to them. Epistemological reductionism fits nicely with Newton's view of scientific interaction, for if we can understand the simple forces that govern basic particles, we can understand reality itself.

TRANSACTION IN PHYSICS

The pull of reductionism marks a crucial watershed between transaction and interaction. Because transaction affirms the full integration of the observer and the observed, it finds nothing inherently subjective about colors or sounds, or inherently objective about physics. The red door, assembled door parts, and swarm of subatomic particles are all equally real answers to different sorts of questions. The traditional empiricist, on the other hand, is committed to finding the one and final reality *in-itself,* independent of any and all observers. This goal drives empiricism toward reductionism, so the question now turns on whether physics actually supports this ultimate, observer-free reality.

Any such attempt must accord with empiricism's fundamental canon— observation. Galileo first challenged the paradigm of self-action simply by observing, without prejudice, the behavior of objects on an inclined plane. Similarly, observing the evolution of modern physics should help us decide whether reality is ultimately reducible to forces and particles. In the 1870s, Clerk Maxwell first noted that the mathematics of statistical probability explains the function of an electromagnetic field better than an aggregate of mechanically interacting particles. In Maxwell's words, "the energy of a material system is conceived as determined by the configuration and motion of the system," not of individual particles. What was previously regarded as the interaction of two opposing forces, action and reaction, became an integral unity, a field. To take either by itself, said Maxwell, is to see "only one side of the *transaction.*"

Maxwell also included light in this new perspective. Newton had speculated that light consists of particles, subsequently called photons. But Maxwell's equations treated light as electromagnetic radiation propagated in waves, a theory Heinrich Hertz confirmed with the discovery of radio waves in 1888. In 1905, Einstein hit upon the novel idea that light could be regarded as either particles or waves, depending upon the nature of the investigation at hand.

Einstein's paper on light was the first of three resounding temblors challenging reductionism and heralding the transactional reconstruction of physics. The second, his theory of special relativity, overturned Newton's idea that relative motion is determined by two constants he called "absolute space" and "absolute time." Newton said the relative speed of anything, including light, should increase as it approaches an observer—just as two trains moving at 50 mph have a relative speed of 0 mph when traveling in the same direction, but 100 mph when converging. Astonishingly, in the late 19th century, Albert Michelson and Edward Morley experimentally proved that Newton's constants didn't hold. Instead, they determined that light travels at the same speed regardless of the motion of the observers. Einstein subsequently declared the speed of light to be invariant, against which even time and space are relative. In short, what classical physics had seen apart as absolute space and absolute time, Einstein saw together as a space-time continuum.

The third shock wave capsized the very idea of matter or mass itself. Interactional physics had replaced the notion of a self-actional inner force with that of particle-masses propelled by energy. But according to the trade-off between velocity and mass ordained by special relativity, any particle approaching the speed of light would also, and impossibly, approach infinite mass. Einstein's ingenious solution, memorialized in the equation $E=mc^2$, is that a light particle can dispense its mass and be regarded as pure energy, and vice versa. Here too, a solution that sees together the interchangeability of matter and energy replaced a theory that saw only energy acting upon matter.

But even Einstein had trouble taking the final transactional step in the science of quantum physics he'd helped create. The problem of space and time resurfaced in subatomic physics when investigators discovered that efforts to determine the position of a particle increased the uncertainty of its trajectory, and vice versa. Here, the philosophical dispute over the reality of things versus relations took shape in this question: Is this uncertainty a product of our limited ability to detect some underlying reality or is the reality in this relational trade-off? In this case, Einstein defended the interactional notion that there must be some fixed underlying fact. Each particle has a determinate position and trajectory, though whatever we use to measure this, even a photon itself, creates a disruption to some degree. A trade-off might be our best approximation of the underlying fact, said Einstein, but this falls short of the reality itself.

Supporting the transactional alternative were the eminent physicists Niels Bohr and Werner Heisenberg. They saw no compelling reason why the microscopic realm must mirror the billiard-ball perspective we experience in the macroscopic world. That each particle has a determinate position and trajectory, and indeed the particulate view itself, is a holdover from interactional assumptions unsupported by observation. For Bohr and Heisenberg, uncertainty is not a consequence of flawed measurements, but a characteristic of the observed field itself. Whether position is refined at the expense of trajectory, or vice versa, depends upon the purpose and interests of the observer.

Generalized as the Copenhagen interpretation of quantum physics, the transactional configuration of position, trajectory, and observer is now the consensus view among physicists. The reality is in the statistical regularities of the field rather than in some unobservable underlying substrate. Probe as deeply as we wish into the structure of the universe, what we see as fact is never separable from the need and interests invested in how we come to know it.

THE RIGHT TOOL

It makes sense that self-action and interaction cast long shadows on the history of science, for they reflect the age-old presuppositions of rationalism and empiricism. Self-action is a natural expression of the rationalistic view that objects conform to mind—that each thing is guided by an inner spirit or life force. Interaction plays upon the opposite intuition, where living and thinking really are just electrochemical reactions to physical stimuli in the external world. Rational self-action weaves a fabulous and comforting tale with a happy ending; empirical interaction pulverizes everything into particles and denies any end or purpose. Is there no middle ground, William James wondered, between being a tender-hearted rationalist and a tough-minded empiricist?

As empiricists, Dewey and Bentley were sufficiently tough-minded. But as radical empiricists, they saw the billiard-ball universe of their predecessors as short on observation and long on supposition. Senses evolved in chasing prey and hiding from predators can hardly be expected to grasp the mysteries of the microworld. Statistical trade-offs and observer-set parameters are what we observe in the practice of physics, so why posit an additional realm of bits and pieces simply because that's how we perceive things in the macroscopic world?

Beyond specific consequences for physics, the transactional stance reflects a new and broader perspective about science itself. Where self-action and interaction hail science as the steady march toward ultimate truth, transaction sees a collection of useful yet fallible human practices open to ongoing modification. This view was bolstered in the 1960s when the influential theorist Thomas Kuhn suggested that science is not a bastion of enlightenment or even of steady progress promoted by reason. Instead, science is a social phenomenon that is piecemeal, halting, and often motivated by expediency. Existing theories typically fall because incongruities amass to a breaking point rather than acceding to superior reason.

Dewey and Bentley were a half-century ahead of the curve in regarding scientific findings not as permanent pillars of light but as makeshift machetes we use to hack at the darkness. Still, they knew they were out of their league in planting the flag for transaction in physics and chemistry. After all, they were philosophers rather than scientists, and thus first to admit that whether, say, the field model in physics is optimal…

> …is not *our* problem, and is not essential to a general consideration of the transactional phase of inquiry. Our assertion is the right to see in union what it becomes important to see in union; together with the right to see in separation what it is important to see in separation.

Like interaction, transaction is a tool for science, not the tool. It is not the business of philosophers to tell scientists when and where to use it. Besides, quantum transactions are a concern in only a very narrow range of investigations. In designing a house or a salad shooter, Newtonian mechanics is preferable on grounds of simplicity and elegance. Other problems also invite us to provisionally break down events into interacting components, while not forgetting a wider transactional perspective. It's useful to view genetic replication as the separation and recombination of basic proteins, while keeping in mind that genes and cells are related to each other and to broader organic functions. We might even imagine life situations where a self-actional stance is beneficial. In plucking up my courage for a dreaded trip to the dentist, I may stiffen my resolve by thinking about courage as an inner resource to be tapped. Or I might pledge to be kinder to my neighbor upon pondering Kant's idea that each person has a unique and unlimited value, while also realizing that persons are forged in life transactions.

TRANSACTION AND PHILOSOPHY

Dewey and Bentley speak from authority on philosophical matters, where they're eager to confront rationalism and empiricism. Rationalism champions the self-actional inner light of mind or soul. Empiricism claims external materials interact with our appearances via perception. In separating mind

Figure 6. **The Transaction of Ideas and Objects.**

In the circuit of inquiry, ideas and objects are interdependent. The bold line below traces the interdependence of object and idea in Dewey's circuit of inquiry.

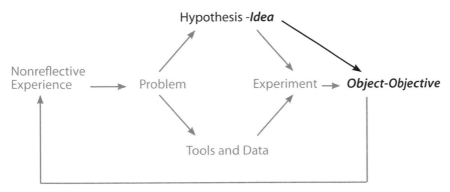

from matter, subject from object, self from world, both alternatives get stuck in the insoluble problem of how a subjective mind gets to mind-independent reality. Both also encourage reductionism. If the world really is all-mind or all-matter, then it's not at all like what we experience.

The radical empiricism of Dewey and Bentley insists we remain true to things as they are actually experienced. We do not conduct our daily affairs fretting, "I'm in here. Hello, world out there. Now how do I get from me to you?!" Typically, we don't even go around aware of distinct objects. Our cognitive headlights are on only intermittently—the default mode of everyday experience is nonreflective. It is only in response to a problem, something anomalous or unusual, that nonreflective experience is shocked into cognitive awareness, where *that* is out of place and *I* must do something about it. Only then do we take stock of what is amiss and potentially useful to restoring order.

This is why the transactional goal is to "see together" what other philosophies "see apart." The paradigm of separate minds and objects yields to a dynamic of problem-solving activity we've called the circuit of inquiry.

As highlighted in Figure 6 on page 41, an object is not a mind-independent existence but an attained *objective* of inquiry. Perceptions and thoughts are not locked away inside a subject—they are hypothetical ideas literally real-ized in such objectives. Mind is not subjective; it encompasses the entire function of *minding* or managing this circuit of inquiry. To anticipate the idea that would consume Dewey and Bentley in the last chapter of their lives, *knowing* as the constructive resolution of problems is integral to anything *known*.

5

Experience and Cosmos

Engaging life from the transactional view is like throwing open a window to the breeze of common sense, a rarity in philosophy. This is a lake. That's a mountain. Up there is a star. They're out there in the real world. I didn't make them. You didn't make them. "Society" didn't make them. They were there before we were here to observe them, and they'll be there long after we're gone. They are not the creations of God's mind or my brain, nor are they a subjective barrier of appearances we dodge and feint to see beyond.

Yet this is not what traditional philosophy calls the common sense view— that things appear to us just as they are in-themselves. To the contrary, for Dewey and Bentley everything just described, "lake," "world," "out there," "past and future," "independence," and even the "I" who does the describing, are attained *objectives* of problem-solving activities. It is the shock of the unexpected that transforms the nonreflective unity of subject and object into the cognitive awareness of things—first to identify the problem and how to deal with it, then to attain the proposed solution by putting it to the test. This is how strangely sparkling expanses became "lakes," how "out there" was set apart from "in here," and how "I" came to find myself as a common thread through each discovery.

Yet many will claim this blurs an important distinction. There is, they say, a crucial difference between *how* we know about things and *what* things actually are. Knowledge, after all, is an epistemological concern about justification. What actually *is*, however, is a metaphysical question about existence. It's one thing to admit the obvious point that nothing is known without a knower, quite another to bite the bizarre bullet that nothing *is* without a knower.

This apparently traps the transactional view in a dilemma. We can either insist that what anything is involves how it comes to be known and arouse the suspicion that, despite our denial, we do make lakes and mountains after all. Or we can accede to the traditional view that things exist as they are in-themselves though inquiry intervenes whenever we say we know anything about them.

Allowing mind-independent existence revives the problem of the external world. But when the alternative seems to be a silly rationalism that sustains the world by thought, even pragmatists tend to cave. Prior to meeting Bentley, Dewey himself occasionally alluded to "bare existences" subsequently "clothed with meaning." But in their working relationship, Dewey and Bentley tolerate no such concessions. A younger Dewey, after all, had declared "what *is* is what it is experienced *as*"—an overt metaphysical claim about existence, not just about knowing. With Bentley's encouragement, an older Dewey finds the renewed courage to do "what I should have done years ago." This is the courage to preach the "radical heresy" that to *be* is to be integrated with problem-solving practices without yielding to subjectivism.

THE HOW AND WHAT OF EXPERIENCE

Faced with the metaphysical challenge to account for what is, beyond what we can know, philosophers have three options. They can keep plugging away at the problem of how mental appearances get to mind-independent reality. They can declare the situation hopeless. Or they can examine the presuppositions that created the problem to find a constructive alternative.

Contemporary realists choose the first option. They keep plugging away at the problem of external reality, confident that new insights into causality or neurophysiology will close the gap between mental events and physical existences. Postmodernists accede to the second, declaring metaphysics in particular and philosophy in general a hopeless enterprise.

Following in the footsteps of Kant and Hegel, Dewey and Bentley pursue the third possibility. By definition, "mind-independent reality" is precluded from "experience" regarded as subjective and mind-dependent. But Dewey and Bentley reject both definitions, engrained though they are in Western thought. Experience, they insist, must be converted from the subjective domain of the knower into a whole inclusive of knower and known.

So far we've focused on knowing as directed inquiry, on the how rather than the what of experience. But experience also encompasses what is, and Dewey takes up this metaphysical question in *Experience and Nature* (1925). Though regarded as his masterpiece, it reads like a transitional work from the hindsight of *Knowing and the Known*—a curious mixture of interactional and transactional descriptions. In the opening chapter alone, Dewey speaks of experience "reaching down into nature," as "penetrating its secrets"—which seem to describe two separate things brought together in interaction. But he also uses experience as an overarching concept: inclusive of what is experienced as well as how it is experienced. And as the chapter builds, Dewey leans upon William James to construct a fully transactional account of thing and thought:

> "Experience" is what James called a double-barrelled word. . . It is "double-barrelled" in that it recognizes in its primary integrity no division between act and material, subject and object, but contains them both in an unanalyzed totality. "Thing" and "thought," as James says in the same connection, are single-barrelled; they refer to products discriminated by reflection out of primary experience.

The traditional view allocates things to the objective natural world and thoughts to subjective experience. But Dewey denies this. Experience includes the natural realm of encountered things:

> "Experience" denotes the planted field, the sowed seeds, the reaped harvests, the changes of night and day, spring and autumn, wet and dry, heat and cold, that are observed, feared, longed for; it also denotes the one who plants and reaps, who works and rejoices, hopes, fears, plans, invokes magic or chemistry to aid him, who is downcast or triumphant.

Experience is thus an inclusive term wherein what we experience is always bound up with how we are able to experience it. The depth of what things are discoverable, says Dewey, is coordinate with a breadth that constitutes inference--the means and methods by which these things become better understood and more useful. There are not, then, separate realms of things and thoughts merely brought together in interaction. Instead one phenomenon, experience, has two intersecting axes, a vertical what consisting of the experienced contents of nature, and a horizontal how comprising the inferential methods that lead from evidence to conclusions. Along these axes, as shown in Figure 7 on page 46, ongoing advances in methods of discovery and communication coincide with a more elaborate and detailed world that is discovered.

Near the convergence of the axes is the inorganic world of mechanical interaction, from microscopic particles to the birth and death of galaxies. Here

Figure 7. **The How and What of Experience.**

How we utilize problem-solving strategies (left axis) is transactionally reciprocal with what can be determined about our world (right axis). Simple schemes of inquiry yield a world more likely to be closed and subjective. An experimental approach helps us see objectively and comprehensively, yet remain open to revision.

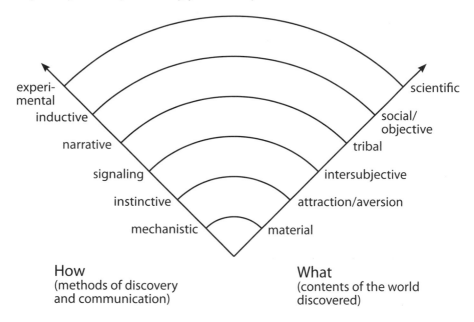

How
(methods of discovery
and communication)

What
(contents of the world
discovered)

there's no worldview, or any perspective at all. This emerges much later, after organic molecules begin to self-replicate and evolution leads to specialization—cells, nervous systems, and eventually brains that function perceptually and cognitively. Animals with sense-perception live in a world of instinctive attractions and repulsions, desires and aversions, but without a centered self or life history from which to project an external world.

The gateway to self-consciousness awaits more developed beings, where learned behavior overtakes instinct and we become aware of ourselves in the expectations of others. At first, the tribal world is inter-subjective and small, immersed in a conversation of gestures with no clear discernment of "I" from "we." Bounded by the terrestrial horizon and that canopy of celestial campfires, this world is animated by the same emotions and desires we feel within us. As gestures become words and words become concepts, the experienced world grows. "Tree" denotes not just this or that tree, but all trees; humanity is not just this tribe, but all tribes. Adventurers return with tales of vast deserts, fathomless seas, and cultures older than the distant memories of their ancestors. The community comes to identify itself and its destiny in terms of the growing narrative it weaves about the cosmos.

Tribes merge, cities emerge. Mathematicians contemplate formulas for infinity; pharaohs and priests build monuments to eternity. Elegant ideas explain it all, but nature wants to reply for itself. Science is born as evidence and observation breaks from restraints imposed by logic or piety. Freed from myths and moral imperatives, nature becomes objective, impersonal. Physical laws of cause and effect govern everything, and we fret about being automatons just along for the ride. Only later do we realize that such laws and causes aren't simply given—we isolate them and set their parameters according to our needs and interests. As transaction overtakes interaction, we begin to understand that nature's reply reflects the perspective and interests that guide our questions.

One transactional relation connects the how and what of experience. Another is found along the extension of each axis. Each broadened perspective brings a new way of thinking about the previous stages. In a tribal and narrative view, for example, matter is regarded as self-actional. Classical physics recasts matter as interacting particles and forces, which later evolves into statistical probabilities within an inclusive field. Each new discovery changed the way people thought about matter, particles, and the world around them. Future scientific findings will continue to require people to alter their assumptions. Dewey and Bentley expanded this sense of process to encompass all kinds of learning and problem solving. According to their view of the how and what of experience, each newly achieved stage reshapes our thinking about everything that preceded it—all the way back to the purely physical realm where the axes themselves originate.

These transactional relations offer a more broadly human view of scientific practices than the reduction of reality to fixed laws and interacting particles. Quantum physics offers breathtaking insights, but it doesn't reduce reality to particles and forces. Instead, it binds the reality of what we discover to the reality of our expanding pursuits and interests. Where reductionism looks for a single point on the continuum marking ultimate reality, transaction finds reality abundant in each phase of an expanding range of relationships.

NATURE IN EXPERIENCE AND EXPERIENCE IN NATURE

More than a decade after writing *Experience and Nature,* Dewey told Bentley that its account of the how and what of experience was "nearer to the unity of knowings-knowns and the transactional than anything I've ever written." Unfortunately, this point was lost among critics who had begun to press Dewey about the relation between experience and nature. Look, they said, there are two alternatives: either nature is in experience or experience is in nature, and neither holds much promise for seeing things in a new, transactional way. For if everything is experience, Dewey must be a rationalist who thinks the world itself is mind-stuff. However, allowing nature beyond experience is to accept mind-independent reality after all, and like any empiricist Dewey finds himself behind the eight ball of the problem of the external world.

Dewey didn't help his cause with explanations that seem to want it both ways. He sounds like a rationalist in exalting the "organic unity" of thing and thought and "external realities as terms in inquiry." On the other hand, talk of "bare" existences merely "clothed" by experience and occasional lapses into "organism-environment *interaction*" does suggest an underlying empiricism and realism.

But a closer look at Dewey's reply to his critics reveals a genuine transactional alternative. In the enigmatic essay "Nature in Experience" (1940), he speaks of a "circle" in which the lessons of nature enhance our methods of inquiry, yet "experience itself" also "contains the processes and operations" that lead to an understanding of nature. To "see together" supposedly irreconcilable separates means neither defending contradictory views nor blending them together into an indistinguishable pulp. It means the ability to draw reciprocal inferences that reveal distinct yet interdependent relations. That's a mouthful, so let's chew it down to size by revisiting the axes of experience.

When we are concerned with the philosophical problem of objectivity—how knowledge of things is possible—it's helpful to begin with the how of experience, experience as the method of problem-solving activity. Any object, in Dewey's famous maxim, is an objective of directed inquiry in the sense that what there is can never be independent of how it is achieved.

Figure 8 on page 49 explores the reciprocal dynamic of what and how. The diagram on the left begins with the philosophical question of how we make sense of the contents of our world. From this perspective we realize that anything we can discern or talk about depends upon our ability to work with and think about it. Recalling that for Dewey mind means minding in this sense, mind-independent reality is literally unthinkable. That cup, that patch of blue sky, that moonlight night, that specimen of allotropic carbon, presents itself as that thing because of efforts we've invested to real-ize what it is. The object

Figure 8. **The Reciprocity of *How* and *What***

In the transactional view, the meaning of "objective reality" depends upon what we want to determine. From a philosophical perspective (figure on the left) we reject mind-independent reality—every object is an objective of inquiry. But with this established, common sense and science (figure on the right) regard these as the public facts of the world.

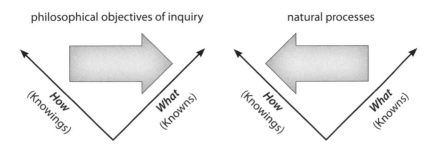

really is that way as a result of such problem-solving activities.

We generalize this ability beyond our individual efforts. Much of what I know I've appropriated from the accomplishments of others. I further believe there are things only experts know, things that as yet no one knows, and even things that perhaps no one will ever know. From the standpoint of how we come to know our world, everything that was, is, or could be known involves knowers. If this is what we mean by experience, then there is nothing beyond experience, though inasmuch as inquiry is unlimited and open-ended there is always a beyond of experience—always more to be known.

As shown in the right-hand diagram on page 49, our perspective changes once we are secure in the familiar world of whats. Starting from there, the problem of what something is becomes a purely empirical question of determining how it came to be. From the standpoint of identifying objects of common sense or science, how is not a philosophical method of objectivity, but an account of the concrete processes that create them. The edge of a sword is forged in fire, not in "inquiry." An ear of corn comes from the planted and harvested earth, not a "hypothesis." In noting that things depend upon the physical processes that make them, transaction should be realistic enough to appease Dewey's critics, for specifically human doings and makings are but an insignificant part of nature as a whole. If experience in this context is the range of what we currently control or influence, then experience is clearly in a natural realm that reaches indefinitely beyond it.

In a nutshell, transaction "sees together" nature in experience as a method of objectivity and experience in nature as physical processes. From these twin perspectives, rationalism and empiricism now appear not so much wrong as incomplete. Rationalism realizes that what there is depends upon how we come to know it, but can't overcome the notion that reality itself is mental or mind-stuff. Empiricism affirms the external and physical nature of what there is, but falters in accounting for how we get to it from our private mental appearances.

Transaction connects these partial insights with a reciprocity of how and what that preserves both the rational method of objectivity and the empirical appreciation of nature. Sufficient groundwork in the how of inquiry yields a beckoning world of objective whats free from skepticism or subjectivism. A secure hold on what we experience frees us to explore how such events occur in nature. The outcome is a world we contemplate with awe, yet transform with our visions and tools.

FROM EXPERIENCE TO COSMOS OF FACT

In retrospect, it was not carelessness or uncertainty that resulted in Dewey's mixed messages about experience, but that the word itself had overflowed its conceptual banks. Our own inventory includes both a philosophical method of objectivity and human makings in a natural world. Confuse this further with rationalism's mind-stuff and empiricism's subjective mental appearances, and experience heads the list of terms in dire need of a makeover.

At about the time *Knowing and the Known* was completed, Dewey wrote a new introduction to *Experience and Nature.* Here he suggests "culture" as a replacement for "experience," a choice clearly narrowed to human endeavors in nature. But a more comprehensive concept was needed for his ambitious project with Bentley, where knowings are fully co-extensive with knowns. After much debate, Dewey and Bentley opt to replace "experience" with the bold word "cosmos," utilizing Bentley's phrase "cosmos of fact."

Cosmos has an odd ring to our ears, since it's come to suggest something a bit loopy and New Age. But the Greek word *kosmos* originally meant a world made intelligible as order is brought from chaos. Cosmos is the root of "cosmopolitan," of being at home in a world in which we actively invest our ideas and practices. In any event, cosmos surpasses experience in unequivocally encompassing "all that is, or can be inquired into." In *Knowing and the Known,* Dewey and Bentley characterize cosmos as…

…nature as known and as in process of being better known—ourselves and our knowings included. We establish this cosmos as *fact,* and name it "fact with all its knowings and knowns included." We do *not* introduce, either by hypothesis or by dogma, knowers and knowns as prerequisites to fact. Instead, we observe both knowers and knowns as factual, as cosmic.

In designating the cosmos of fact, Dewey and Bentley also insist upon a transactional interpretation of fact—that what is known as fact is inseparable from how we determine it to be so. In support of this, Dewey and Bentley cite the original Latin root of fact, *factum,* as "something done or made." The cosmos of fact, accordingly, is inclusive of knowing and the known—the how and what of the encountered world.

A LIST OF FIRM NAMES

Just as *Knowing and the Known* went to press, Dewey looked back at *Experience and Nature* as an attempt to explain what difference "the words metaphysics and metaphysical would make *on* experiential grounds, instead of on the ground of ultimate Being behind experience serving as its underpinning." With experience now recast as the cosmos of fact, Dewey's metaphysical intentions become clearer. The epistemological claim that objects are objectives of inquiry is now supplemented with Dewey's metaphysical assertion that the experienced world is the real world, and not some supposed existence in itself beyond experience in us.

At the end of *Knowing and the Known* is a "trial group of names" now "firmed," to cite Dewey's and Bentley's expression, by transactional analysis. This glossary is intriguing, for it offers a pithy summary of semantic dos and don'ts in philosophy and the behavioral sciences.

Some words are deemed to be beyond rehabilitation. "Reality" heads this pack as the "most obnoxious" metaphysical misnomer. "Epistemology" must be avoided where it "directly or indirectly assumes separate knowers." Other names, including "existence," "object," and even "nature," are troublesome outside of carefully specified transactional context—"context" itself among the items on the list!

As successor to "experience," "cosmos of fact" now shoulders the burden of "seeing together" what other approaches tear apart. Whether it's elastic enough to close the gap between thing and thought, knowing and known, remains to be seen.

6

Transaction and Sign-Behavior

"Of all affairs," wrote Dewey, "communication is the most wonderful." The ability to express meaning emerged from a complex web of emotions, needs, and habits. Long before the evolution of language, humans shared their dreams and desires through what Dewey's friend and colleague George Herbert Mead dubbed a "conversation of gestures." Dewey was so convinced we create ourselves in social acts that he called this "the inclusive philosophical idea." Rationalists can delight in the solitary lighthouse of reason, empiricists in parlays for pleasure or power. Dewey believed we ineluctably cast our fate with one another.

WHAT'S IN A NAME?

What goes on when humans use names to identify things? Surprisingly, some of the bloodiest hand-to-mind combat has been joined over this question. The traditional rationalist view is captured by a story Bill Cosby used to tell about Adam and Eve naming animals in the Garden of Eden:

"That's a sparrow," says Eve.

"That's a rabbit," Adam contributes.

Eve pauses as a squat mammal with a long snout waddles by. "That's an aardvark," she says at length.

Adam is curious. "Why an aardvark?"

"I don't know," Eve replies. "It just looks like an aardvark!"

We're amused because it's silly to say an animal Eve has never seen "looks like" a word she's never used. The anecdote illustrates that the connection between sounds and things may be initially quite arbitrary. But Cosby's yarn does tap a long-standing presumption that naming bonds language to the essence or nature of things. "Aardvark" doesn't just refer to this or that animal, but to the very essence of being an aardvark. It holds for all aardvarks—past, present, and future. As described by the philosopher Ludwig Wittgenstein (1878-1951), in this view, objects are like exhibits in a museum, each identified by an accompanying plaque. We learn about things by reading the plaque and connecting the name to its corresponding specimen.

Empiricists are justifiably suspicious of "essence" and "inherent nature," spooky words with no scientific pedigree. Modern behavioral psychology, pioneered in the first half of the 20th century by John B. Watson (1878-1958) and B. F. Skinner (1904-1990), claims that even "consciousness" is the fading echo of these outdated beliefs. Perceptually stimulated brains produce neuromuscular reactions we observe as behaviors. But there's nothing we can empirically assert as consciousness in addition to these physiological events. Behaviorism, as developed by Watson and Skinner, restricts psychology to the observation and interpretation of human behavior. The study of sign use should presume nothing beyond the correlation of stimuli with verbal and motor responses. Behaviorists are interested in *conditioning*—how various stimuli produce predictable reactions in subjects.

Though equally suspicious of any autonomous mental realm, for Dewey and Bentley behaviorism goes overboard in reducing organic activities to the performance of body parts. This, they wrote, is especially evident in the study of speech, where

> Watson's isolation of language—naming as physiological processes of vocal organs—is a fine example of the grossest kind of neglect of the transactional. He didn't even get as far as environmental *inter*-action.

SIGN-BEHAVIOR

What behaviorism misses, though it's plainly observable, is the importance of language to human activity that is purposive and directed. Signs link latent tools, abilities, and resources to desirable outcomes in problem-solving situations. Citing an example from pragmatism's founder, Charles S. Peirce, Dewey has us consider the significance of a drill sergeant commanding recruits to "present arms." The sign, a verbal command, is neither a fixed name on a plaque nor the mere passage of air over vocal chords. Instead, it connects a skill the recruits have acquired to a goal deemed desirable on this occasion. In lowering the butts of their rifles to the ground in unison, a cognitive concept has found fulfillment in a concrete existential outcome.

Dewey and Bentley regard sign use as meaningful behavior that *does* something in the world. Consider the simple sentence "Maria runs." In the traditional view, "Maria" is a particular term contained within the class of "running things" designated by the predicate. But a transactional approach replaces this static containment with the dynamic idea of inference—the ability to behave in ways that modify an environment. "Running" is a behavior that enhances what we know about Maria and her awareness of her own agency. It's nested within a matrix of learned social abilities by which she acquires her sense of self, including her goals and expectations. Even when entrenched in habit and no longer thought about, "running" remains a behavioral option for dealing with future challenges and opportunities.

Though Dewey and Bentley insist their philosophy of transaction is behavioral, it is not the narrow behaviorism of Watson and Skinner. Instead of reducing behavior to bodily gestures and vocal sounds, they insist that it be interpreted broadly:

> …behavior is always to be taken transactionally, i.e., never as *of* the organism alone, but always as of the organism-environment situation, with organisms and environmental objects taken as equally its aspects.

Just as "field" replaced the paradigm of discrete particles and forces in physics, in linguistics, sign-behavior has supplanted the old view that signs are like nameplates or that language merely expresses preformed thoughts. Critics of behaviorism, such as Claude Lévi-Strauss and M. A. K. Halliday, came to see language, behavior, and culture as inseparable. Some, like the philosopher-linguist Noam Chomsky, now insist that language is essential to thought itself. Dewey and Bentley not only anticipated these advances, but saw well beyond their present development. Unlike Halliday and Lévi-Strauss, who regard language and culture as in the natural world, and Chomsky, for whom language aptitude is in the brain, Dewey and Bentley see brain, sign, culture, and nature engaged in interdependent organism-environment transactions that transform ourselves and our world.

KNOWING ABOUT NAMING

Epistemology is the study of knowledge, of how we know what we know. How particular things acquire their names is a matter of lexicography—the

Figure 9. **Naming-Known as Designation and Existence**

The Dewey-Bentley theory of sign-behavior builds upon the transactional insight that anything in the cosmos of fact that exists and can be named (left) is linked to the function of naming or designating it (right).

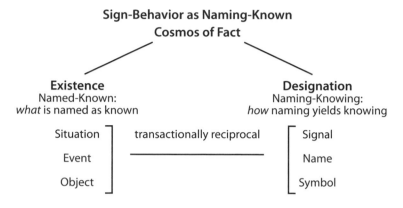

study of the development of meanings over centuries of social use. Less abstract than epistemology, but more concrete than lexicography, is the theory of signs, where we determine what can be known about the naming process itself. Dewey and Bentley consider a bewildering list of relatives among knowing and naming, but here's a recap of the primary ones.

1. Knowing-Known: Epistemology, the study of knowledge
2. **Naming-Known: Theory of Sign-Behavior, to know about naming**
3. Naming-Named: Lexicography, how things acquire names

We've already explored the first relation, the epistemological co-determination of knowing and knowns as the how and what of inquiry, and Dewey and Bentley were not targeting lexicographic stories about the historic evolution of names. Accordingly, they focus on Naming-Known—what we can know about naming-behavior.

Figure 9 on page 56 is a composite of Chapters V and VI of *Knowing and the Known*. The overarching cosmos of fact reminds us that what is or can be known is always bound up with how we come to know it. Dewey and Bentley call this what and how, respectively, *existence* and *designation*. Existence is the "known-named phase of fact, transactionally inspected." It broadly encompasses physical, psychological, and behavioral facts, but resists the lure of mind-independent reality that would suppose "both a 'something known' and a 'something else' supporting the known."

Under existence on the chart are degrees of precision Dewey and Bentley distinguish as *situation, event*, and *object*. The least exacting of the three, situation, merely takes in a "general scene or background." An object, on the other hand, is a fact in sharp cognitive focus. Between these, and acting as a kind of broker, is event. An event emerges when a situation becomes eventful—that is, when the onset of a problem demands that elements of a situation be brought into focus with the objective of resolving it. Situation, event, and object correlate with nonreflective experience, problem, and objective in Dewey's method of inquiry.

As an illustration, Dewey and Bentley invite us to consider the Parthenon in circumstances where situation, event, or object is the dominant mode. A local cab driver may experience little more than an impending source of traffic congestion—a situation that doesn't even become eventful if the cabbie is habituated to taking an alternative route. An executive caught in gridlock and late for an important meeting endures a stressful event, with perhaps no resolution yet in sight. An anthropology student entering the Parthenon for the first time may be awestruck by its significance—something truly event-*ful*. She's determined to pursue the objective details of its architecture, art, and history.

Coordinating with existence on the chart is *designation,* the general term Dewey and Bentley select for the how of naming-knowing. Paired with the three levels of increasing precision in existence are *signal, name*, and *symbol* under designation. Signals are behavioral and social, but precommunicative. When a bird senses a predator and takes flight, the commotion stimulates other birds to follow suit. But they are not actually communicating with each other, not sharing a meaning or intention. At the other end of the spectrum, symbols are signs with meanings so abstract they no longer refer to specific objects. While indispensable to mathematics and formal logic, such symbols are peripheral to the social function of sign-behavior that concerns Dewey and Bentley.

Accordingly, it is *name* under designation they single out for further study. As shown in Figure 10 on page 58, naming-behavior includes, in order of increasing precision, *cue, characterization*, and *specification*.

Unlike mere signals, cues are genuine acts of communication, epitomizing what we've called the "conversation of gestures." Though often associated

Figure 10. **The Specification of Name**

Dewey and Bentley choose Name under Designation for additional development. Naming-behavior ranges from simple gestural cues and everyday characterizations to the technical specifications of the natural and social sciences.

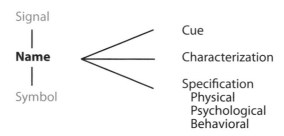

with situations—the raised hand of the traffic cop may prompt the cabbie to seek an alternate route—cues also play an important role in events and desired objectives. A sign to steal home flashed to a base runner or the inviting glance of a lover are clearly conscious, eventful, and goal oriented. Characterization, write Dewey and Bentley "…includes the greater part of the everyday use of words" adequate to common or practical purposes. Everyday problems and options for resolving them engage the names and descriptions of characterization. Specification, they add, is "…the most highly perfected naming behavior, best exhibited in modern science." The student's plan to systematically study the Parthenon or the scientific designation of water as H_2O are typical examples of specification, which includes the technical terminology of the physical, psychological, and behavior sciences.

CIRCLES OF TRANSACTION

At least in part, Dewey's followers have shied away from *Knowing and the Known* because its detailed theory of signs seems contrary to his famous disdain for systematic philosophy. What, they ask, is the point of dissecting and diagramming sign-behavior? Why not leave such details to linguists, anthropologists, and behavioral psychologists—experts with specialized training and a wealth of empirical data?

The greater value of the existence-designation system is not in its choice of categories, but in the insistence that these are *transactionally* interrelated. As philosophers, distinct from social scientists, Dewey and Bentley are tracing out the idea that what we know is inseparable from how we come to know it.

Its central theme is that anything within the cosmos of fact is both an objective existence and the outcome of the problem-solving activity by which it is known.

Let's revisit the existential terms situation, event, and object. These are not simply whats—distinct kinds of existences. Instead, they also reflect how they function in progressive phases of problem-solving activity. A situation that does not become an event remains a nonreflective having—a double-barreled unity with no discrimination of thing or thought. An alertly grasped object is either connected to a hypothesis to be tested or is the outcome of such a test. There is no ultimately right or real determination of existence, but rather different reals reflecting different levels of cognitive engagement.

Across the diagram, it's equally clear that how we use signs depends on what we want to accomplish. In everyday situations, where problems are routine, we invest minimal cognitive energy by way of signals, gestures, and common descriptive characterizations. It is the uncommon, the recalcitrant, that demands the brow-furrowing specification that leads to a sophisticated new object, a new objective what.

POSTULATION

The postulate of immediate empiricism reminds us that all experienced things are equally real. Fright at a sudden noise is just as real as the subsequent realization that it was only a window shade tapping. Some indigenous cultures use apricot seeds to treat cancer, whereas we rely upon surgery or chemotherapy. I swear by duct tape in plumbing emergencies, whereas my wife is partial to a plumber with a welding torch.

Though reality isn't at issue in such cases, usefulness or efficiency certainly is. I really was scared, but discovering it was only a window shade tapping shows that my fear was unfounded. Homeopathic treatments have an organic wholesomeness, but cancer is serious and prompts staying with confirmed medical practices. The desirability of a dry basement trumps my vanity as I grudgingly call a plumber.

In working out how specification arises from common terms, Dewey and Bentley agree that explanatory efficacy is vital to sign-behavior. Where self-action hopes for the manifestation of an internal essence and interaction is fixated upon cause and effect, transaction approaches efficacy in terms of inferential breadth—the explanatory reach of a theory to related but more limited practices. Rather than innate powers or invariant laws, transaction looks to explanations that are reliable and broadly applicable, yet eminently revisable.

The intrigue of such comprehensive conceptions actually goes back to Peirce, who called them "guiding principles." In the *Logic,* Dewey refined this notion by envisioning a linked set of propositions that, "like rungs in a ladder," progress from specific applications to a "leading principle"—the governing scientific concept. How far one must ascend the ladder depends upon the problem at hand. Consider, for example, the properties of electromagnetism. An electrician building a circuit may only need to keep in mind that a current is equal to potential divided by resistance. A physicist, on the other hand, knows this current is further explained as a charge differential between nuclei and electrons. By and large, the electrician functions well on a relatively low rung, though the problem of, say, capacitive interference in bundled wires, might demand a step or two up the ladder. But the physicist knows that the same phenomena that light a lava lamp are manifest in gyroscopes and the aurora borealis. One's position on the ladder is a matter of being properly positioned for the job at hand, not of finding "reality." At the same time, the uppermost rungs offer synoptic views, optimal "seeings-together" that appear fragmented from lower positions.

In their search for transactional terms in *Knowing and the Known,* Dewey and Bentley worry that "principle" suggests the odd notion of some final or absolute fact. As such, they prefer "postulation" as the conceptual aim of specification. "Postulate" has the flexibility of suggesting or trying out, and "postula*tion*" reminds us that a directed action or how is implied in any determination of what. Consequently, postulation is the anticipated prize as we move from characterization to specification, and from more limited to more advanced levels of specification.

Dewey and Bentley thus affirm the importance of leading principles. But unlike philosophical realists, who yearn for an ultimate top rung denoting true reality, they are happy climbing up and down an indefinite progression of rungs. Realists are right to declare that the view from the upper rungs is breathtaking, but for this very reason, the thought of an end or limit is deflating. Instead, with diligence and effort we climb to the farthest rung we can see, then to the farthest beyond that. These highest-reached rungs are postulations that put lower rungs into perspective and sort them into discernable groups, yet nothing in the history of scientific progress or a transactional worldview posits an end to the climb—an ultimate reality that terminates inquiry.

In *Knowing and the Known,* Dewey and Bentley supplant the analogy of a ladder with that of a cluster. Meanings overlap and pervade one another. Names are firmed or clarified not in isolation, but within a cluster of related terms.

> Names are, indeed, to be differentiated from one another, but the differentiation takes place with respect to other names in clusters; and the same thing holds for clusters that are differentiated from one another.

Think of a cluster of associated names as planets circling a central star representing a postulation. Planets closer to the star are brighter and more visible; others are more massive and have a greater gravitational effect upon the system. Both are specifications that stand out among less prominent characterizations and cues. The influence they exert on the system is real, as is that exerted by the postulation upon them. So the water that slakes my thirst, keeps my lawn healthy, and reflects the scattered spectra as a blue lake are all instances of H_2O. Indeed, H_2O is a common fact that explains each of these other properties—features that would remain dissimilar and unconnected without it. Similarly, the Parthenon of the distracted cab driver and the harried manager *is* the historic artifact of the engaged student, whose broader understanding includes reasons why it attracts traffic.

Each, however, remains a distinction of usefulness, integration, and explanatory power. Just as no planet is more real than another, there is no privileged meaning expressing the ultimate reality of water or the Parthenon. Utility, after all, can be measured only within a context of use. Just as a planet can be too massive for the useful function of sustaining life, it would be silly to say the Parthenon is really just calcium carbonate. Though explanatory power tends to increase as we ascend the hierarchy of specification, the bright central star in one system may be a marginal white dwarf in another.

7

Life Transactions

Imagine it is 1859, the year of Dewey's birth. There's no electricity, scant indoor plumbing, and getting to town involves hitching up a buggy. Now fast forward to 1952, the year of his death. This is an age of rockets, televisions, and block-long computers. Dewey lived through five major wars and nine cycles of economic boom and bust. A case could be made that his life spanned the most technologically explosive period in the history of civilization, even considering the intervening six decades.

Dewey was amazed by these marvels, but also alarmed. Like many others, he was deeply concerned with what has become known as the crisis of modernity—that science and technology outpace the moral developments needed to channel them responsibly. Miraculous advances in transportation, communication, and medicine promise an earthly utopia. Hydrogen bombs, overpopulation, and poor stewardship of the earth are portents of self-obliteration. Because facts have traditionally been isolated from values, those who create these technologies typically deny responsibility for their effects. The moral leadership expected of churches, schools, pundits, and parents is comparatively diffuse, enervated, and conflicted.

Inasmuch as our very survival is at stake, it's natural to suppose that contemporary ethicists, in particular, would be eager to weigh in on solving the crisis of modernity. This has not happened, however. For the most part, specialists in ethics and moral philosophy have either been ineffectual or have actually taken up crowbars that widen the gap between scientific and moral institutions.

EMPIRICISTS UP TO NO GOOD

Let's consider the crowbar wielders first, whom Dewey identifies as the empiricists of his day. By the 20th century, scientific empiricists agreed that spooky talk about essence and substance had become an embarrassment to philosophy. To be meaningful, they insisted, any factual assertion must be observable or testable.

Since there's no test for being, souls, or mind-stuff, metaphysical claims are pure nonsense. Though we might not lose sleep over the demise of metaphysics, empiricists had wrestled a second, and more prized, victim onto their chopping block. Moral language, they insisted, is also meaningless. Good can't be weighed on a fish scale; evil can't be tracked by its bloody footprints. Because there is no objective test for moral judgments, ethics is as worthless as metaphysics.

Since most of us make moral judgments and regard them as important, these empiricists realized they had to explain what's really going on in such pronouncements. One account, offered by modern utilitarians, is that meaningless moral claims can be translated into meaningful statements about personal preferences. So, for instance, the meaningless phrase "peace is good" can be translated into assertions such as "I like peace" or "I prefer peace" that can be verified by measuring the speaker's pulse rate or pupil dilation.

More austere empiricists, known as emotivists, find even this too lenient. Meaningless moral dictates cannot be translated into statements of preference, for they are *expressions* of such preferences. "I like peace," they say, is just the emotional release of a noise—"peace!"—that *is* the expression of the preference.

Despite this difference, utilitarians and emotivists have the same bottom line. Moral language is literally nonsense, a holdover from an age when words held magical powers. The moral claims of individuals are really physical acts and reactions measured by behavioral psychologists. Values are really cultural habits and customs recorded by social scientists. As with metaphysics, ethics becomes a relic of pre-scientific thinking forever banished to the tower of babble-on. Modern empiricists don't just use the crowbar to separate facts from values, they smash values to smithereens.

Dewey agrees that empiricists are justified in divesting moral language of its special magic—there's nothing sacred or hallowed in such assessments. In his view, however, they continue to see apart what should be seen together, and thus miss the significance of moral discourse in our lives. In limiting values to mere statements of preference, empiricists confuse a starting point with an end or goal. We have basic biological desires, of course—for food, shelter,

Figure 11. **The Circuit of Valuation**

In the transactional view, the circuit of inquiry helps procure values as readily as it determines objective facts. Moral deliberation over a problem does not directly yield a value, but rather a value candidate that can tested much like any other hypothesis.

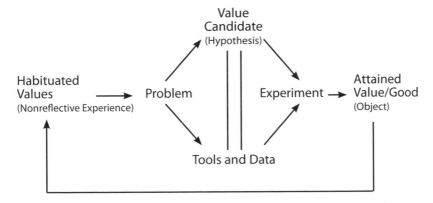

security, etc.—which Dewey calls "impulses." But only a child, or perhaps an empiricist, would mistake these for values. "I want it! I want it!" expresses an impulse or preference—something desir*ed,* but not necessarily desir*able;* something valu*ed,* though by no means valu*able.*

Is this just a lot-of-*ble*? Perhaps, for those who say objective descriptions have nothing to do with morality. But for Dewey the objectives or facts attained by directed problem solving activity are equally values or goods. After all, an aqueduct that solves a water shortage and a medicine that cures a disease are both factual and valuable.

Recognizing the difference between what we happen to value at the beginning of inquiry and what proves to be valuable at its end, Dewey distinguishes a *value candidate* from a genuine *value* or good. As shown in Figure 11 above, these have the same function in moral discourse that a hypothesis and its attained objective have in determinations of fact:

Despite shifting the emphasis from fact to value, from what *is* to what we *ought* to do, the story is familiar. Practices that lubricate social relationships build the fund of values acquired when we're young and only occasionally need to question thereafter. They direct our impulses to appropriate behaviors: I want the whole cake, but I *ought* leave some for others. This toy is mine, but I *ought* to let you play with it. It is only when impulses conflict, when I'm inclined to do something not socially sanctioned, that preferences come under scrutiny and I ask myself, "What would happen *if* I do this or that?"

When the imagined outcome defeats such impulses, I reaffirm the original norm without further reflection. But when doubts stick, moral deliberation is necessary. I must ask myself whether what I like, desire, or value *really is* like-able, desirable, or valuable. To determine this requires a test reflecting not just my present likes and dislikes, but the long-term interests of everyone affected by such an action, including myself. It requires, in other words, that a value candidate demonstrate its credentials as a genuine social value or good—not just a preference, but the end result of a process of valuation.

In contrast to this circuit of valuation, modern empiricism retains an inter-actional outlook. It can detect and measure conflicts among competing prefer-ences. It can advise those in authority how to manage impulses to encourage socially sanctioned behavior. But empiricism can't integrate these preferences and impulses with achievable goods. Without the transactional tie between value candidates and such values or goods, it lacks the capacity for authentic moral deliberation.

THE IOUs OF RATIONALISM

Despite their thinning number, or perhaps because of it, modern rationalists have become increasingly strident. Not without justification, they accuse empiricists of gutting ethics and abetting the decline in public morality. They swear to remain stalwart, however, as champions and protectors of the Good. There are moral absolutes, standards of right and wrong that shine like beacons to all of sufficient purity and devotion. Rationalists vow to solve the crisis of modernity by slaying the dragon of relativism.

But if the good is so luminous, why is there so much disagreement about it? Plato claims the ultimate good is the Form of Good. Judeo-Christian and Islamic traditions insist it is the will of God. The English philosopher G. E. Moore (1873-1958) says we just know what's good when we encounter it, the moral equivalent of, say, seeing the color yellow. Kant avows it is dutiful ac-tion to what we know to be right. Why does each version of rationalism have its own vision of good?

For Dewey, there's no mystery. In each version of rationalism, the good is so lofty it's clean out of sight! Too noble to be fully grasped by frail and faulty folks like us, it must be interpreted by sacred texts, confessors, or moral system-builders. The good is up there in the clouds, say the rationalists. You can't quite see it, but we can. Here's a promissory note, an IOU. Trust us. Obey us. We're in with the good. We'll put in a word for you.

That rationalists don't deliver the good is perhaps most evident in Plato and Western theology. No one now believes the natural world is merely a copy of ideal forms. It took only one generation for Aristotle to object that form and matter are united in physical things. And while some brave souls still insist that reason alone can fathom God's plan for creation, most agree this is best left to faith or revelation. "Through a glass darkly," Paul says of our mortal efforts to understand divine justice, only "later face to face."

Moore's answer seems refreshingly different. The good isn't some distant sanctified star, but right here in front of us. Bad is as plain as our clucking tongues and wagging fingers. It's easy to see his point when thinking about heroic sacrifices or heinous murders. But is good as obvious as yellow, or is there something to the old saw about shades of gray? Is capital punishment right or wrong? Should motorcycle riders be required to wear helmets? Is it wrong to steal medicine I can't afford for my gravely ill child? If we suspect that morality often involves deliberation and discussion, weighing options and considering consequences, Moore's assurance that good is as plain as yellow seems not just naïve but dangerous. For when we don't just see good, surely there are experts with superior vision more than happy to tell us what to do. Again we're left with a promissory note.

For Kant, the only thing that is always good is a good will—having good motives or intentions. Achieving positive outcomes is also nice, but consequences vary. The desire to do the right thing, however, remains good even when things turn out badly.

To test whether any proposed act is morally permissible, Kant devised a maxim called the categorical imperative, which promises an automatic way to tell right from wrong. We don't have to appeal to God or any other moral authority. Instead, we need only the ability to recognize simple contradictions.

For any contemplated act, the categorical imperative asks us to consider what would happen should this act become universal law—a fancy rehashing of every mother's mantra: "What if everybody did that!" If an act becomes impossible should everyone do it, then it is morally impermissible. If not, then it is morally permissible. So, for example, if everyone lied all the time, everyone would realize they're being lied to and no lie would work. If everyone had to kill everyone else, soon we'd all be dead and killing would be impossible. Lying and killing are thus shown to be immoral. On the other hand, helping others in times of need could go on indefinitely, since the supply of folks troubled by problems seems inexhaustible. Charitable acts, accordingly, pass the categorical imperative and are morally permissible.

Since it appeals to reason and is personally verifiable, Kant's moral objectivi-sim has a clear advantage over rivals dependent upon authority or intuition. It stumbles, however, when prescriptions conflict. What should I do, for example, when the only way to save someone's life is to lie to his would-be murderer? Good intentions are fine, but we must also consider options, worry about short- and long-term consequences, and perhaps choose the lesser of two evils if need be. If everyone did that, we'd all think and act more like pragmatists.

Whereas empiricists see ethics interactionally, as stimuli and responses, rationalists remain self-actional. Good is an emanation of the divine will, intuition, or reason. Even the categorical imperative now seems like one more comforting authority, an excuse to avoid the effort and anguish typical of moral deliberation.

RESOLVING THE CRISIS OF MODERNITY

Philosophy's contribution to the gap between science and morality is now clear. Empiricists deny the existence of good. Rationalists praise it so highly it's pushed clean out of sight. Transactional pragmatists agree with empiricists that we do have preferences, and with rationalists that some things really are prefer*able.* But it sees these together. A value candidate that demonstrates its worth gains recognition as a genuine value. Pragmatic goods are not absolute or final, but outcomes of trials and tests that have proven their enduring ben-efits, though revisable when new problems arise.

As things improve, so too do the methods that improve them. More than a half-mile high, the Burj Khalifa in Dubai is both a jaw-dropping skyscraper and the realization of a new buttressed-core technology that may soon support buildings twice its height. In our progression from entrails-sorting to Doppler radar, *how* we approach problems has transformed our world as assuredly as *what* we have achieved through such transformations. We currently lack, however, an adequate method for integrating technology and morality. Ac-cording to Dewey, this widening gap can't be closed unless the responsible application of the method of inquiry becomes common to both. His bottom line is stark, direct, and eminently transactional: Scientific institutions must become morally responsible; moral institutions must become scientific.

It is no longer acceptable to say, "I design the bomb, let others decide how to use it," or "Clear-cutting is more profitable than selective harvesting, let oth-ers worry about preserving the ecosystem." To recognize, instead, the integral correlation between facts and values means that those who create and apply new technologies are responsible for their long-range consequences.

In insisting that moral institutions become more scientific, Dewey is not talking about fundamentalists with iPhones or Twittering jihadists—these are in ample supply! Instead, he means that core beliefs should be regarded experimentally: as vital and formative, yet also revisable—followed because they demonstrate their value across the board and not just because they are hallowed traditions or divine decrees.

TRANSACTION AND THE BEHAVIORAL SCIENCES

According to Dewey and Bentley, the behavioral sciences lag behind the natural sciences in the transition from interaction to transaction because the relationships they study are comparatively complex. Human behavior is less predictable than the activity of water molecules or a colony of ants. It is thus not surprising that psychology, sociology, and political science have lagged behind physics and chemistry, both in terms of discoveries made and the methods used to attain them.

Even where a transactional appreciation of relational webs is emerging, it is often mixed with self-actional and interactional ways of thinking. Perhaps this is most evident in psychology. Behaviorism reduced mind and meaning to a series of marks and sounds. The alternative proposal by Sigmund Freud (1856-1939) jumped to the opposite extreme. To his credit, Freud recognized the significance of the unconscious behind the perceptive-cognitive ego and the moral super-ego. He backtracked to self-action, however, in regarding this as an inner self, an irrational id he dubbed "a cauldron full of seething excitations." Instead of a transactional circuit of nonreflective experience, problem, and cognitive object, where the settled and unseen provide resources for the known and seen, Freud conjured clandestine wars among isolated structures. In advancing the idea of a collective unconsciousness underlying the individual psyche, Freud's successor Carl Jung (1875-1961) introduced a positive social alternative. But even he regarded these formative myths and legends as hidden "archetypes" rather than behavioral guides and tools.

On the whole, anthropology and sociology have fared better. At the turn of the 20th century, many agreed with the eminent social psychologist G. Stanley Hall (1844-1924) that non-Western cultures were "adolescent," in need of nurture and guidance. The groundbreaking field studies of Franz Boas (1858-1942) and Margaret Mead (1901-1978) helped create a more egalitarian and pluralistic view where every culture is a test case in the art of living. Transaction views social evolution as a spectrum of ongoing experiments.

It is one thing to "see together" from the shelter of the study, quite another to work for this in the rough and tumble political realm. Dewey would be discouraged that public policy is still largely adversarial rather than experimental—dominated by ideological struggles rather than hypotheses forged by consensus and checked by consequences. The power and promise of democracy, as he saw it, means more than toeing a party line or rubber-stamping the plans of experts. Instead, it implies the informed involvement of everyone affected by the consequences of policy decisions.

Dewey admired the form of democracy exemplified by the New England town hall, where citizens forge public policy through give and take. The one who wears the shoe, he liked to say, knows more about where it pinches than experts or central planners. This is not to deny the usefulness of professional advice, or that some programs and policies are properly administered at the national level, but even these should involve the deliberations of what he called the "great community"—decisions informed by the outcomes of local and regional trials. Urban investment zones, charter schools, wetlands preservation, and sunset laws that expire unless renewed are examples of national investitures that began as local experiments.

Dewey's commitment to democracy is based on the realization that our world is a mixture of the stable and the precarious. We count on the stable resources of nature to promote security and prosperity. But the precarious, the dangerous, is both inevitable and unpredictable. Things go wrong in ways not anticipated by engineers and experts. This is why, says Dewey, we benefit from the widest range of views. The solution may lie with the voice from the wilderness, the misfit, the crackpot.

Democracy as full participation requires a commitment to basic freedoms. Dewey construes such freedoms broadly, inclusive of both freedom *from* constraints to participation and freedom *to* be able to take advantage of opportunities. Freedom *from* oppression includes familiar Bill of Rights protections—of thought, expression, assembly, religion, control of capital, etc.—deemed vital to democratic action. Freedom *to* full participation includes opportunities afforded by education, health, meaningful employment, and social enfranchisement. Dewey regards freedom *from* and freedom *to* as transactionally inseparable.

To many, the idea that a society can be more experimental than adversarial seems hopelessly naïve. Dewey harbors no illusion that this is achievable without basic changes in our approach to education. He rejected the still prevalent belief that student success is measured by the ability to recite blocks of information or to perform well on standardized tests. Instead, he envisioned an educational system that inspires innovation, cooperation, and experimentalism. Children are naturally playful and curious. Educators can channel these impulses in directions that are constructive and rewarding. The "three R's" and other skills are introduced along the way—not as ends to be mastered for their own sake, but as means to achieving successful outcomes. At least as important as knowledge is the *habit* of welcoming problems as opportunities for growth. Education should be a lifelong commitment to innovative engagement, not something terminated with the acquisition of a certain set of skills. In this, says Dewey, resides the hope of preparing citizens for effective democratic action.

TRANSACTION IN ECONOMICS

I once took a college course in economics and recall being terrified by the blackboard-bending equations the professor used to introduce the topic. Economics employs models and statistics that track the production, distribution, and consumption of goods. More fundamentally, economics is about human behavior and about what we are willing to risk in pursuit of the things we value. In other words, economics engages the same moral questions that philosophy paints with a broader brush.

So long as care of our immortal souls was the chief social objective, the church deemed the material needs of common folk venial and unimportant. According to Dewey, this allowed early economists such as Adam Smith (1723-1790) to fly under the radar of kings and clergy. Economics was the first human science to tie empirical observation to quantitative methodology. By the second decade of the 20th century, it was more advanced and predictively reliable than psychology, anthropology, or sociology.

But was it more transactional? The great battle of 20th-century economics pitted progressive John Maynard Keynes (1883-1946) against free-market champions Ludwig von Mises (1881-1973) and Friedrich Hayek (1899-1992). Keynes rejected the idea that prosperity is determined solely by the marketplace of supply and demand. Instead, he argued, government should proactively increase demand by redistributing wealth to increase the purchasing power of workers and stimulating the economy by spending freely in times of recession. Von Mises, to the contrary, decried meddling with the natural forces of supply and demand and the threat to individual initiative posed by the welfare state.

Dewey and Bentley did not live to see the social consequences of this debate. However, beginning in the 1950s their transactional experimentalism was applied to economics by E. C. Harwood, founder of the American Institute for Economic Research (1900-1980). Though Harwood respected the impact of Keynes and von Mises, he thought they both leaned too heavily on intuition and too lightly on experimentation and observed consequences. For Harwood, a Keynesian "proof" is really a dialectical sleight of hand: "Here is my story about the Keynesian revelation; next, I verify it by writing it in [mathematical] shorthand; finally, I prove it beyond doubt by drawing a picture of it." In general, writes Harwood, Keynesians judge "the usefulness of a theory by its plausibility instead of by checking its implications against measured economic changes."

Though more sympathetic to von Mises' free market views, Harwood finds his methodology even more rationalistic and self-actional. Unlike natural science, which deals with objective facts, von Mises regards social science as "systematically subjective." Economic first principles are divined solely from "reason unaided by experience." Citing Dewey's observation that "reason pure of all influence from prior habit is fiction," Harwood concludes that relying upon such introspective truths is a "leap backwards to Platonic idealism"—the antithesis of knowledge as a tool for prediction and adjustment.

According to economist D. Wade Hands, Keynes and von Mises represent a widespread tendency among economists to fall back upon "3x5 card basic principles"—supposedly self-evident economic truths that reveal a correct set of policies and practices. Adages such as "values are preferences," "individuals maximize utility," and "firms maximize profit," are basic precepts of what we now call neoclassical or orthodox economics.

Dewey, in contrast, paddled the headwaters of a more variegated watershed that became known as institutional economics. Where the classical tradition stressed the utility function of the individual, the institutional alternative embraced a transactional spectrum of social phenomena—laws, norms, technologies, language, and the distribution of wealth. Iconoclast economist Thorstein Veblen (1857-1929) chided capitalism for wasting on showy status symbols profits that should be reinvested. Clarence Ayers (1891-1972) encouraged entrepreneurs to challenge the barons of inherited wealth and power. More broadly, John Commons (1862-1945) looked for equitable ways to mediate disputes among diverse interests in a democratic society.

By mid-century, institutional economics had fallen from favor because it was considered too scattered, too speculative, and insufficiently rigorous. Advances in mathematics and statistics addressed the concern about simplistic utility calculations, and Keynesianism took up the fight for social justice. Economists who worried that these approaches still relied upon 3x5 card thinking—*a priori* assumptions about human abilities and motives—regrouped under the banner of new institutional economics.

This view retains the insight that choices reflect an array of social influences; but it accepts the neoclassical tenets that scarcity leads to competition and choice is relative to anticipated costs. In the real world, individuals have limited information and mental capacity, so decisions incur costs in the form of risks. Institutions are important because they embody rules that lessen the uncertainty of these risks. Individuals with common interests form organizations that learn how to take advantage of the rules in order to survive. Though none are perfect, stable institutions emphasize the rule of law, civil liberties, and flexibility in accepting reform. For the new institutional economics, the effective integration of institutions, individuals, and organizations is the key to prosperity.

Another branch of economics approaches transaction from a formal and quantitative frontier. Econometrics "sees together" empirical data, mathematical statistics, and economic models. Though introduced nearly a century ago, econometrics has come into its own in the past four decades because of breakthroughs in methodology and computation. Economists construct models to make sense of conditions that are dauntingly complex in the real world. Ideally these could be determined by controlled experiments, the way scientists isolate particles or pathogens. But human subjects resist being squeezed into bubble chambers or flasks, so economists rely upon data to confirm their hypotheses. The theory that scarcity affects price, for example, can be checked by tracking the price of orange juice in the aftermath of a crop-destroying freeze.

Though good enough for rough assessments in simple cases, such correlations break down under exacting needs and complicated conditions. Granted that whenever factor x is present we always observe consequence y. What *other* factors might produce y, and what is the degree of their influence? There was no hope of precision about this until the mid-1970s, when economists including David Hendry and Christopher Sims began to develop new econometric strategies. Instead of thinking in terms of causal relations among a restricted set of factors, Hendry's model begins with a range of "plausible" variables subsequently narrowed to those that cohere with one another and the expected outcome—a winnowing that simplifies the model and makes it more predictive. Sims' approach is freer still, subjecting a virtually limitless array of data and histories to whittling techniques that utilize massive computations and advanced software.

In addition to its holistic approach to relations, theoretical econometrics has additional transactional virtues. Where the traditional notion of cause and effect simply assumes that the past determines the future, these new models include human expectations among the data. Because hopes and fears about what *will* happen affect present events that *do* happen, the future affects the past as surely as the past affects the future. Past and future, in other words, are reciprocally interdependent. Moreover, instead of wholly determinate facts produced by strict causal interactions, an econometric model incorporates uncertainty and probability into its very structure. Borrowing a page from Niels Bohr and Werner Heisenberg, uncertainty is not just our inability to know the so-called underlying reality; instead, the reality *is* uncertain to some degree. Like transactional pragmatists, most contemporary econometricians don't regard their models as "true" or even "correct." Instead, they regard them as helpful tools or abstractions that, by design, are flexible and revisable.

Despite these considerations, econometrics remains controversial even within the profession. All this mathematical wizardry has not significantly improved our ability to predict broad economic trends. Some theorists regard these models as reliable only for short-term forecasting. Others say recent advances make them increasingly applicable to policy planning and long-range goals. Though the latter claim has merit, we should remember that policies arise from deep-seated institutional values. These rules and norms shape the very design of econometric models, including the data we load into models and our evaluation of results. Because current values are built into our models, we can't expect them to predict how these values will evolve and the social changes they'll bring. As useful as econometrics may be, there is no magic formula that obviates the give and take of democratic action Dewey calls social intelligence.

Ultimately, then, we are reminded that facts and values are intertwined and that knowledge is not a starting point, but an achievement of experimental action. To assert, for example, that the market system is better than centralized planning is ultimately not a matter of intuition, causal reasoning, or the statistical analysis of data. Instead, it begins with public discussion of the expected benefits of current policy, checked against actual consequences, and compared to alternative approaches. Nor is self-interest a manifest axiom of human nature. In the heyday of the robber barons, "good" business meant the self-actional aim of unlimited personal enrichment. Later, this was modified by an interactional corporate model where management maximizes profit for shareholders.

Today a widely discussed transactional alternative, stakeholder theory, explores business models that extend consideration beyond shareholders, employees, and customers to people in the greater community whose interests are affected. Besides a basic appeal to fairness and equity, advocates point to practical advantages of the approach such as building goodwill and avoiding regulatory entanglements. As economist Gianfranco Rusconi puts it, it's just a "good idea" to assume that "company survival and development is conditioned upon an awareness of everyone involved in some way."

UP AROUND THE BEND

You can ponder perpetual motion,
fix your mind on a crystal day.
Always time for good conversation,
there's an ear for what you say.
— John Fogerty

In proclaiming the virtue of tolerance, our founding fathers pitted themselves against the self-actional blinders that refuse to countenance any end other than *my* God, *my* country, or *my*-self. But tolerance, as "live and let live," is still inherently interactional. It falls short of a genuine transactional pluralism of individuals experimenting with abundant social, aesthetic, and spiritual options. For Dewey, participation in a truly viable democracy involves reciprocal commitments. The freedom to create personal values and goods incurs the obligation to leave a surfeit of constructed goods. The transactional citizen aspires to be an "involved innovator" or "engaged entrepreneur," receiving and giving in equal measure.

If these musings sound naïve and utopian, Bentley would not be surprised. He predicted that a full appreciation of the transactional view would take generations. Currently, there isn't enough cognitive scaffolding to connect present realities to transactional possibilities. From the struggle and strife of the world as it is, we can barely imagine what such changes would amount to. We do know that in this experimental outlook, the difference between hypotheses and consequence can be great. We know, further, to expect the unexpected. Even if we achieve our ends-in-view, we might be disappointed at the outcome. We might even need to revisit basic assumptions of transaction itself, or look for a successor.

Dewey was not the kind of optimist who believes things *will* get better, but a meliorist who allows only that they *can* improve with concerted effort. Hopeful enthusiasm tempered with patience epitomizes the transactional outlook. The roots of transaction spread slowly, tentatively, leaving ample room for other ventures, other experiments.

And yet, they do spread. In their lifetime, Dewey and Bentley saw transaction become the dominant methodology in chemistry and physics, and the progress they observed in genetics and biology continues to this day. Neurophysiology and psychology have advanced beyond self-actional brain states and interactional behaviorism to an organic integrity of mind-environment. Entirely new sciences, such as ecology and ergonomics, have been created on expressly transactional postulations.

As Dewey and Bentley also forecast, progress has been slower in the social sciences. Education is still fixed on rote memorization and standardized tests rather than the synoptic problem-solving that worked so well in Dewey's Chicago school. Economics is just now outgrowing the dialectical manipulation of 3x5 card first principles. In politics, consensus building evaporates like steam from the cauldrons of domestic partisanship and international brinksmanship.

The passing parade is all hugely entertaining—until, that is, we think about the unresolved crisis of modernity: the prospect of self-annihilation should we fail to integrate a humane view of science and technology with an experimental approach to values. We can't work together until we begin to *see* together—not some preconceived *what,* some universal good, but a common *how* that is experimental, inclusive, and pluralistic. The philosophy of transaction Dewey and Bentley sketch in *Knowing and the Known* is a template, an invitation, left for us to shape, refine, and try out in the social as well as the natural sciences. Our survival, let alone our dreams, may depend upon whether or not we accept this challenge.

Subject Index

value candidate, 65-66, 68
Veblen, Thorstein, 72

W

Wagner, Adolph, 3
warranted assertion, 7, 9, 64
Watson, John B., 54-55
Wittgenstein, Ludwig, 54

Provide reliable lifetime income for you and your family by supporting AIER's mission

"Make all you can, save all you can, give all you can."—John Wesley

AIER's tax deductible planned giving program offers a lifetime income plan for up to three generations. Imagine being able to have a guaranteed income for you, your children and grandchildren, and support the work of AIER in the process.

Since 1969 donors' to AIER's programs have enjoyed the advantages of having their assets managed by AIER and the security of knowing that AIER will provide income for life to their designated individuals. Most organizations are not willing to commit themselves to a program that will not benefit them for 75 years or more; for us this is simply a part of our long-term commitment to helping individuals protect their financial future.

AIER offers qualified donors many attractive benefits, including:

- Federal and state income tax deductions
- Capital gain tax savings on gifts of appreciated assets
- Annual income for life or a designated term
- Transfer cash, securities or other property including buildings and land
- Reduced probate costs and estate taxes
- Expert asset and investment management
- Support of AIER'S work and mission

We will be happy to run simulations on our planned giving programs to help with your decision. We will be happy to run simulations on our planned giving programs to help you with your decision. It is very important that you consult with legal and financial advisors before committing to such deferred gifts. As a nonprofit research organization, we can offer information and simulations that can help you make these decisions, but we may not provide specific legal or financial advice.

Call the Development Department at 413-528-1216 or info@aier.org for more information. You can also run simulations at:
http://www.aier.org/support/planned-giving/calculator